CW00765133

CANAL BOOKS

A guide to the literature of the waterways

by

Mark Baldwin

M & M BALDWIN
London
1984

© Mark Baldwin, 1984

ISBN   0 947712 00 3

All rights reserved. No part of this publication may be reproduced or transmitted in any
form or by any means, electronic or mechanical, including photocopy, recording, or any
information storage and retrieval system, without the written permission of the publisher.

Published by M & M Baldwin, 98 Kenyon Street, London SW6 6LB
Distributed by Shepperton Swan Ltd, The Clock House, Upper Halliford, Shepperton,
Middlesex TW17 8RU
Printed by C.I.Thomas & Sons (Haverfordwest) Ltd, Merlins Bridge, Haverfordwest

CONTENTS

FOREWORD
by Charles Hadfield

Canal Books is its author's first published book, first product of a new publishing house, and first on its subject. It is also packed with hidden treasures.

If only I had had it in 1938, when I began to collect canal history, buying my first three books from the Oxford University Press library in London: Vernon-Harcourt's *Rivers and Canals*, Willan's *River Navigations*, and an American, Roberts' *Middlesex Canal*, in the intervals of also collecting the red-haired librarian. I bought many others during the London blitz, when booksellers were glad to sell cheap today what might be burned tomorrow. Enquiry often brought from a lower shelf a book long pursued or, more often, never heard of. Two out of the three editions of *Bradshaw* came thus.

Graftons, transport specialists, opposite the British Museum, were the Mecca of many war-time pilgrimages. The shop, managed by a railway enthusiast called Peddie, had several dozen canal books, pamphlets and Acts recorded on worn slips. There in 1938 I had bought my Priestley, and there every few leave days I balanced my exiguous cash against the encircling temptations, before carrying my purchase to lodging or river fire station to read and re-read.

Acts...I remember my pre-blitz incredulity when I found that some early Acts were still on sale from HMSO. On the spot I bought all four of my favourite canal, the Grand Western. Then Hitler removed the stocks. Pursuits...I stalked Jackman's *Transportation* the length of Britain, someone else always getting it first, until – O joy! – I netted it. How evocative *Canal Books* has been, though chastening too. South's *British and Irish Waterways Gazetteer*? I've never heard of it. Frisi's classic of 1762 in English translation? I didn't know.

Mark Baldwin has done scholars, librarians and enthusiasts great service; and I believe has enjoyed doing it.

PREFACE

Collecting canal books is a pursuit which becomes more common, although I can hardly envisage it being as popular as, for instance, collecting books about railways. It is, however, a larger field than many realise; if, as throughout this book, we include river navigations within the term 'canals', it goes back over 350 years to John Taylor, the 'Water Poet', whose *A New Discovery by Sea* (1623) describes a boat journey up the Hampshire Avon, and contains suggestions for its improvement. In fact, as the systematic improvement of rivers for navigation goes back several hundred years before that, the literature can be said to extend over five or six centuries. For practical purposes, though, the collector will be unlikely to find much before about 1650. He should be able to afford, without too much difficulty, late seventeenth-century Acts of Parliament, and books and pamphlets such as Andrew Yarranton's *England's Improvement by Land and Sea* (2 parts: 1677 and 1681).

So much for depth – but what of breadth? Here the collector must decide for himself what to pursue, but breadth is on offer. Even without fiction, our shelves may boast books by Arnold Bennett, C.S.Forester, A.P.Herbert, and Robert Gibbings. Including fiction brings Anthony Trollope, Thomas Love Peacock, and Ngaio Marsh within our grasp. If we depart from the straight and narrow path of collecting books, we may develop all sorts of strange tastes – canal postcards, stamps, share certificates, boat engines, even teapots – but the purist need not fear; I shall not discuss such aberrations at length.

Having been a canal book collector for many years, and (with my wife) having dealt in canal books for six years, I am very conscious of the lack of any real guide to the literature. Our customers frequently find our catalogues genuinely educational in that they describe books which are not listed elsewhere. The collector, however, needs something more than booksellers' catalogues; this book aims to answer that need. More than a mere listing, it discusses about 400 books, giving some idea of their value, both cash and contents. For a more rigorous bibliography, turn to *Canals – A New Look. Studies in honour of Charles Hadfield*, to be published by Phillimore & Co in August 1984. Amongst other delights, this lists about 700 books on waterways in the British Isles, published in or before 1950, and about 80 books and articles describing cruises on European waterways before 1939.

Even a book as modest as this one needs friends. I am therefore happy to record my debt to Penny Beck, Pippa Burton, Charles Hadfield, Hugh McKnight, Roger Squires and Sue Wright, all of whom have gone out of their way to assist its birth. The British Museum kindly supplied the photograph of the circular Manchester Ship Canal medallion; all the others are by the author.

A Note on Values

This is not intended to be a price list, but I feel that to give some guide to the cash value of the books mentioned will lend it extra interest. I have therefore appended a Grade letter to almost every printed item referred to in the text, but not to the 'hardware' discussed in Chapter 8. In interpreting these values, please remember:

(a)   The prices are estimates of what a buyer might have expected to pay in 1984 to acquire a complete copy of the original edition in reasonable condition from a specialist or good-quality second-hand bookseller.

(b)   Older books vary in condition more widely than newer ones. There would be a considerable difference in price between two copies of an eighteenth-century book, if the first had spent two hundred years in a country house library, snuggled down crisply in polished calf, whereas the second had spent its days more usefully on the shelves of a lending library, victim of the thumbs of all comers, possibly being rebound a couple of times and thus losing its virginity and its margins. I have tried to give prices for 'average' condition, though I shrink from defining it.

The Grade letters used are:

A	up to £5	E	£50 to £100
B	£5 to £10	F	£100 to £200
C	£10 to £20	G	£200 to £500
D	£20 to £50	H	over £500

For books which do not fit neatly into these ranges, pairs of consecutive Grade letters are used.

Chapter 1

CRUISING & CRUISING GUIDES

I imagine that most readers of this book will have had their interest in canals aroused by a cruise. If this interest blossoms, one of its early expressions will probably be the search for books about the canal or river on which this initial cruise took place. It is exciting to read of other people's experiences in traversing routes you know yourself, especially if several accounts can be found spanning a longish period of time. For certain waterways, like the Thames and the Broads, dozens of cruises have been described in print; for others, such as the River Wey or the Caldon Canal, you will be lucky to find one or two journeys described. It is true that many of the earlier waterway guides were compiled from cruising logs, but books written specifically as guides are dealt with later on in this chapter. Also, some early works of fiction describe waterway travel so graphically that we must assume that their authors had had personal experience of boating, but further discussion of these will be left to Chapter 7.

Accounts of Cruises

Many early travels by waterway weren't really what we now think of as cruises, since the travellers were merely using part of the public transport system of their day – the packet boats. Typical of these are John Carr's trip from Athy to Dublin in 1805, described in his *The Stranger in Ireland* (1806 – Grade D). The packet boat system was particularly well developed in Ireland, and several canal companies even built hotels for the accommodation of canal travellers. An English trip of comparable date may be found in *Journal of a Governess 1807 – 1811*, edited by Edward Hall. The governess was Ellen Weeton, whose extensive series of journals and letter books has survived only in part, and remained unpublished until 1936. (This is Grade D, and the David & Charles facsimile edition is Grade CD.) She describes a packet boat trip on the Leeds & Liverpool Canal, undertaken to visit relatives, which shows how packet boats allowed reasonably quick and comfortable journeys to be made by those who could not afford the higher fares charged by the stage coach operators.

Many travel books of the period 1770 – 1850 contain brief but illuminating descriptions of packet boat travel, and a useful review of what is so far known of these services is contained in Hugh Malet's article 'The Packet Boat Age', published in the *Journal of the Railway & Canal Historical Society* for July 1981.

In contrast to the canal packets, early cruises using privately owned or hired craft were usually on rivers, or on the waterways in the flatter lands of Eastern England. Thus William Gilpin writes of his trip down the Wye in 1770 from Ross to Monmouth in *Observations on the River Wye* (1782 – Grade E), a popular book which reached its fifth edition in 1800. A few years later a Fenland trip was made by Lord Orford, but the account was not published until 1868, when *Lord Orford's Voyages round the Fens in 1774* (D) appeared, edited by John Childers. Perhaps the earliest book devoted entirely to a cruise is by 'The Water Poet', John Taylor, who described a lengthy journey in *John Taylor's Last Voyage, and Adventure...in which he past, with a Scullers Boate from the Citie of London, to...Oxford, Gloucester, Shrewsbury, Bristoll, Bathe...* (1641 – Grade F). There being no canals at this time, he was obliged to hire a 'waine' to get the boat from one river to the next. While describing the portage between the Churn and the Frome, he remarks that by a short canal 'Stowd [sic] and Churne might be cut into one, and so Severne & Thames might be made almost joyned friends'. He returned to London after seven weeks, recording that by

> 'lesse than twenty dayes labour 1200. miles were past to and fro in
> most hard, difficult and many dangerous passages, for the which I
> give God most humble and hearty prayse and thankes'.

Not bad for a man of 61, even remembering that he had a crew of two men and two boys.

In 1866, John MacGregor's *A Thousand Miles in the Rob Roy Canoe on Rivers and Lakes of Europe* (see Chapter 5) was published, a highly successful book which was continually reprinted for 30 or 40 years. The author had a typically Victorian mixture of self-confidence, determination, invention and industry, strongly shot through with philanthropy. He instigated a number of charitable schemes, including that for employing some of London's street children in 'The Ragged Shoeblack Society'. In 1865 he had designed a touring canoe, and the skill with which he handled both the canoe and the publicity generated by his book laid the foundations of the modern sport of canoeing as we know it. His enthusiasm was infectious, and spread through his newly founded Canoe Club, so that within a few years we find adventurous canoe trips being undertaken all over Europe, and beyond. In Britain, many rivers were too short to provide satisfactory cruising by themselves so, inevitably, canoeists went from river to river by canal or by sea. Several books resulted, though all are scarce nowadays. These include *Canal and River: a canoe cruise from Leicestershire to Greenhithe* (1869 – Grade D) by 'Red Rover' (still unidentified), George Heaviside's *Canoe Cruise down the Leam, Avon, Severn and Wye* (1871 – Grade D) and Thomas Holding's *Watery Wanderings 'mid Western Lochs* (1886 – Grade D). Another anonymous work, *The Waterway to London, as explored in the "Wanderer" and "Ranger"* (1869 – Grade D) describes a three-man trip by skiff and canoe from Manchester to London via the Bridgewater Canal, Mersey, Ellesmere Canal, River Perry (by virtue of a portage to this tiny stream passing under the canal), Severn, Gloucester & Berkeley Canal, Stroudwater, Thames & Severn, and Thames. This took three weeks, with a number of memorable incidents including a horrible portage across a mile of mud between the Mersey and the Bridgewater Canal (to avoid a six-mile row in tidal water). To compensate for this, the transit of Sapperton Tunnel sounds delightful:

> '...the glimmer of a dip, placed in the bunghole of the Ranger, gave us courage to enter. Once in, we could see the other end shining like the point of a pin, at a distance of two miles and a quarter...The canal was of a uniform depth of three feet, with a sandy bottom, and as clear as crystal. When we emerged at the other end we really appeared to be floating on air, the water was so perfectly limpid that one could scarcely see it.'

Despite the advent of power cruising, canoeing continues to be a popular method of exploring waterways. William Bliss was perhaps the leading twentieth-century waterway canoeist, and his *The Heart of England by Waterway; a canoeing chronicle by river and canal* (1933 – Grade D) takes us along many of the 'mainline' waterways of England and Wales. *Rapid Rivers* (1935 – Grade C) describes a number of his river trips, and some by canal, e.g. the Brecknock & Abergavenny. His canoe journey with the poet J.C.Squire was described by the latter under the title *Water-music, or a fortnight of Bliss* (1939 – Grade B). Their route was from Oxford to Warwick by canal, thence down the Avon to Stratford, by rail to Cricklade, and back down the Thames to Oxford. The book is rare in first edition, being more easily found as *Solo and*

Duet (1943 – Grade A), a double volume containing *Water-Music* together with another of Squire's English travel books. Sadly, Squire seems to have been less keen on canoeing than was Bliss, and provides fewer navigation details than we would now wish for. Bliss has been followed onto the water by thousands, but although numerous books on canoeing technique and canoe-building have been written, I can think of no-one who has followed Bliss into print to portray the delights of this gentle, silent means of travel (no-one, that is, describing cruises in Britain).

CANAL AND RIVER;

A CANOE CRUISE

FROM

Leicestershire to Greenhithe,

INCLUDING

A GUIDE TO THE THAMES BELOW OXFORD,

BY

RED ROVER.

" Ye glittering towns, with wealth and splendour crowned ;
Ye fields, where summer spreads profusion round ;
Ye *streams*, whose vessels catch the busy gale ;
Ye bending swains, that dress the flowery vale ;
For me your tributary stores combine :
Creation's heir, the world, the world is mine ! "

BEDFORD :
PUBLISHED BY ROWLAND HILL & SONS.
—
1873.

LEFT: George Smith, and his book, in *Two Girls on a Barge*.
RIGHT: An early canal cruise, by an anonymous author.

In 1891, V.Cecil Cotes wrote the first full-length book to describe a trip by converted narrow-boat. The journey from Paddington to Coventry on *Industrious* is well described in *Two Girls on a Barge* (CD) which also has some excellent line drawings. The boat, plus crew, was hired from Corbetts, and temporary cabins built in the hold. Although certainly based on an actual journey, the book is not presented in a straightforward non-fiction style. For instance, the party met the canal reformer George Smith (see Chapter 3) but although describing his book

10

Canal Adventures by Moonlight, including a picture of him, and mentioning a gift inscribed 'Mr. Right Door Smith', Cotes refers to him throughout as 'Mr. Gershom'. Why?

We are fortunate that a competent professional writer has left an account of a long canal voyage. E.Temple Thurston hired Eynsham Harry and his boat for a month, and the resulting book, *The "Flower of Gloster"* (1911), is without question a highlight of canal literature. The better bindings of the first edition (D) have a fittingly attractive appearance, their handsome green cloth bearing a gilt narrow-boat, and the text is complemented by numerous pencil illustrations by W.R.Dakin. I confess I'm less fond of the plates of Dakin's water-colours, and am more appreciative of the photos which, long preserved by Mrs. Thurston, were published in the facsimile edition by David & Charles (1968 – Grade B).

The book describes Thurston's progress from Oxford via Stratford-on-Avon, Tewkesbury and Gloucester to Inglesham. His prose is memorable, he paints an evocative picture of rural England before the First World War, his photos show he spent time on or by canals, yet doubts have been raised as to whether the trip actually took place as described. It seems possible that the book was put together from a number of shorter cruises, towpath walks and encounters (see David Blagrove's article 'The "Flower of Gloster" – fact or myth?' in *Waterways World* December 1972). Nevertheless, this book deserves a place on every canal bookshelf, and is in short supply despite editions in 1911, 1918, 1968 and 1972.

For the next account of a narrow-boat trip we have to wait another twenty years, when Wilfred Byford-Jones took a party from Wolverhampton to Llangollen in the horse-drawn *Neptune*, and included a brief account in *Vagabonding through the Midlands* (1935 – Grade B). Canvas partitions divided the hold into several cabins, and one is not surprised to read that several groups of boatmen regarded the party with 'amused interest', for the men were dressed 'in flannels and coloured shirts open at the neck and the girls in beach pyjamas of striking patterns'. These 'jolly Bohemians' danced to Cuban numbers played on a portable gramophone. This is all much more in the tradition of Thames and Broads boating, and yet, despite Byford-Jones' obvious ignorance of canal life and his patronising attitude to the boatmen, a few interesting facts are recorded. I particularly value his description of the boatmen trolling for pike from the moving boats, a practice I don't remember seeing mentioned elsewhere, certainly not in any of the modern books about boatmen. Thus even a lightweight book may provide a fresh detail.

In 1944 comes the most famous of all narrow-boat trips: *Narrow Boat* (B) by L.T.C.Rolt. Reprinted in various editions in 1945, 1946, 1948, 1949, 1978 and 1980 (all A or B), this is a book which thoroughly deserves to be kept in print. Once part-owner of a garage, Tom Rolt turned his back on the commercialism of the motoring world of the late 1930s, bought *Cressy*, and re-converted her at Tooley's yard in Banbury, intending to live aboard as a professional writer. He had difficulty in finding a publisher for *Narrow Boat*, but let us be thankful that he persevered, for its publication led to the formation of the Inland Waterways Association, without which today's canal scene would look very different. As a direct result of *Narrow Boat*, Tom Rolt, Charles Hadfield, Frank Eyre and Robert Aickman met in Aickman's flat in 1946, and founded the IWA. These four became Secretary, Vice-Chairman, Treasurer and Chairman respectively. Ironically, within five years, both Rolt and Hadfield (and many more besides) had been expelled from the IWA, and Aickman's account of the meeting, written thirty years later, doesn't even mention Hadfield by name. Hardly *Cressy*'s fault, I know, but remember, when reading *Narrow Boat*, how it all turned out for its author. Particularly poignant is his description of parting from *Cressy*, which occurs at the end of the second volume of his autobiography *Landscape with Canals* (1977 – Grade A).

As soon as the British Waterways Board started selling off narrow-boats in the mid-1960s, conversion of working craft for cruising became widespread. Many such have been described in magazine articles, and occasionally in book form, e.g. John Poole's *Narrow Boat Venture* (1975 – Grade A) which recounts the conversion and cruising of *Barrhead*, a steel boat originally built for the Grand Union Canal Company.

Cruises in pleasure boats on the Thames and the Broads have a solid history of a century or more. Amongst the former are Mrs. R.S.De Courcy Laffan's *The Cruise of the "Tomahawk"* (C) published as a paperback in 1892, Joseph and Elizabeth Pennell's well illustrated *The Stream of Pleasure. A Narrative of a Journey on the Thames from Oxford to London* (1891 – Grade C), Frank Morley's *River Thames* (1926 – Grade C) describing a boat trip from Cricklade to Gravesend by canoe and converted ship's lifeboat, and Robert Gibbings' *Sweet Thames Run Softly* (1940 – Grade B), delightful both in its gentle prose and its numerous wood engravings. A rewarding look at Thames

12

pleasure-boating in the last century is provided by Reg Bolland's *Victorians on the Thames* (1974 – Grade B) which contains a good selection of period illustrations from Canadian canoes to the most extravagantly ornate houseboats of the day.

On the Broads, a rather more adventurous approach was developed by the Victorians. The very nature of the Broads, largely lock-free and set in a flat landscape, encouraged sailing holidays, thus permitting some of the excitement of sailing without the danger and discomfort which can be experienced by coastal yachtsmen. The earliest Broads cruise I've come across is described in Walter White's *Eastern England, from the Thames to the Humber* (1865 – Grade D) in two volumes. About a hundred pages of the first volume are devoted to a cruise on the Broads, and a shorter section in the second volume to one on the Waveney. By the end of the century, cruising guides abound, and many cruises were written up, e.g. Anna Dodd's *On the Broads* (1896 – Grade C), Henry Doughty's *Summer in Broadland* (1889 – Grade CD) which went into six editions, and P.H.Emerson's *On English Lagoons: being an account of the voyage of two amateur wherrymen on the Norfolk and Suffolk Rivers and Broads* (1893). Emerson was a leading photographer of Broadland, and his books are now highly regarded for their artistic, photographic, social and waterway interest. With such competition, it is not surprising they're expensive, if and when you can find them. The best way to sample Emerson's work is to consult his biography *P.H.Emerson, photographer* (1974) by P.Turner and R.Wood.

Some intriguing glimpses of the style of the Broads yachstmen can be derived from the adverts found in the guides; the larger yachts were often described as being fitted out with wire spring mattresses, tip-up basins, electric bells, and pianos, and having experienced crews, who are 'honest, sober, and obliging'. At the other end of the scale, 'young men who lounge in a nude state on boats while ladies are passing...may be saluted with dust shot, or the end of a quant'. Although still popular, Broads cruising has produced few interesting books since those of Arthur Patterson, a Broadland enthusiast whose works include *The Cruise of the "Walrus" on the Broads* (1923), *Through Broadland by Sail and Motor* (1930), and *Through Broadland in a Breydon Punt. By "John Knowlittle"* (1920), all of which would be Grade C.

As distinct from the Broads and the Thames, canal cruising by pleasure boat was virtually unheard of during the nineteenth century. A notable exception is J.B.Dashwood's *The Thames to the Solent by canal and sea* (1868). This is Grade D, but is available at Grade A as a facsimile reprint published by Shepperton Swan. It describes a trip in a Una boat from Weybridge to Lymington via the Wey & Arun Canal, and is graced by a number of charming drawings including one of Buz, a Pomeranian which accompanied the author and his wife.

It wasn't until the twentieth century that canal cruising in purpose-built craft (other than canoes) started to develop, and amongst pioneering works are Carey John Aubertin's *A Caravan Afloat* and Peter Bonthron's *My Holidays on Inland Waterways*. Neither is dated, but both were published in 1916. The former describes a number of trips in the author's ungainly craft – a box-like cabin 17ft long, mounted on a punt-styled hull 33ft by 6ft 6ins. Its original propulsion was by paddle, driven via pedals and a chain by the rapidly tiring legs of Carey John or one of his crew. In due course the machinery was abandoned and the boat was towed by horse or man, poled, rowed or paddled. In this way Aubertin navigated many of the Midlands canals, and wrote most entertainingly of his travels; the book well deserves its revival as a Shepperton Swan facsimile (1981), as original copies are now hard to find, and would be Grade D.

Bonthron, alas, can not be described as an entertaining writer, but the interest of his tersely written book lies in his extraordinary perseverance in tackling such a large number of waterways. Not confined to using one boat, and hence to the connected waterway network, Bonthron used all sorts of craft, often sent by rail from Salters of Oxford, to explore as many waterways as possible. Bank Holiday after Bank Holiday, he clocked up the miles, not just on the Thames and the canals of the Midlands, but on such widely separated waterways as the Royal Military Canal and the Caledonian. The book is written in the self-satisfied style of a man who has achieved his target of navigating everything within reach. Despite its lack of literary merit, it was popular, probably being used as a cruising guide, and went into three editions by 1919, all of which are Grade CD.

Other early cruisers include Austin Neal, whose *Canals, Cruises and Contentment* (1921 – Grade D) is part log, part advice. He rather overdoes the latter, devoting, for instance, a whole chapter to 'Washing-up'. The cruising section describes two long trips: Derby to Llangollen and back (340 miles) and Derby to Oxford and back (380 miles). T.W.Cubbon also deserves mention here for *The Wizard Dee: a June Voyage from Bala to the Sea* (1934 – Grade D) and especially for *"Only a Little Cockboat": roughing it from Dee to Severn and canals between* (1928 – Grade D). The title of the latter was the term used by the boatmen to describe Cubbon's small camping boat.

Later years have seen an expanding number of books recalling cruises, of which the following is but a selection. Hugh Malet's *Voyage in a Bowler Hat* (1960 – Grade B) is a most readable tale of a single-handed voyage from London to Ellesmere Port in the 16ft dory *Mary Ann*. At Ellesmere, the *Mary Ann* was loaded onto a coaster and shipped to Dublin, from where Malet crossed Ireland by waterway. Ireland also proved attractive to Tom Rolt, whose lengthy boat journey is recalled in *Green and Silver* (1949 – Grade C). David Owen has given us a trilogy: *Water Highways* (1967), *Water Rallies* (1969), and *Water Byways* (1973), all Grade A. In these he describes the numerous trips he has undertaken in his own boat, which have extended to most of the connected waterway system of England and Wales. Incidentally, the last chapter of *Water Rallies* reviews the literature of canal cruising over the past two hundred years, and may be read with considerable pleasure, even though it is not very thorough in its coverage. Roger Pilkington, though preferring waterways on the European mainland (see Chapter 5), has written two books about cruises on the Thames and its connecting waterways, both Grade B: *Thames Waters* (1956), telling of the trial runs of his newly converted *Commodore*, and *Small Boat on the Thames* (1966), in which the newly built *Thames Commodore* covers much of the same ground, before going off to further adventures across the Channel.

By this point I hope that most readers will have found something which refers to their home waters or favourite cruising ground. Certainly, I have not attempted to be comprehensive, but to show something of the range of books which have been written, and which may still be sought from bookshops or libraries. There are many more I know of, but haven't mentioned, and doubtless many of which I have no knowledge. Boating magazines also provide many accounts of cruises – for instance Donald Maxwell's 'A Motor Boat's Discovery of the Upper Medway' in *Yachting Monthly*, published in three parts in the issues of February, March and April 1913. Other sources include *Motor Boat* (later *Motor Boat & Yachting*) and the earlier issues of more general magazines, such as *Bazaar*, *Field* and *Country Life*. In addition, there are doubtless as yet unknown boating logs, still in manuscript form. One such was the diary of an extensive tour made by a Mr. Farrant and his friends in 1873. Their route was Oxford–Napton–Warwick, down the Avon to Tewkesbury, thence to Gloucester, via the Hereford &

Gloucester Canal to Hereford, down the Wye, by rail to Bristol, and home to Oxford via the Kennet & Avon Canal, and the Thames. This interesting log remained unpublished until 1977, when it appeared under the title *Rowing Holiday by Canal in 1873*, published by the Oakwood Press. By some strange coincidence, Howard Williams and four friends took an almost identical route in 1875, and his diary also remained unpublished for a century. It has finally seen the light of day as *The Diary of a Rowing Tour from Oxford to London* (Alan Sutton, 1982) – a title which doesn't prepare you for the actual itinerary, which was much the same as Farrant's, except for a tow from Chepstow to Bristol, and the final leg from Reading to London. There must have been other rowing tours on other waters, so presumably more diaries lie undetected in attics or trunks, awaiting re-discovery.

Waterway Guides

Apart from books like those by Phillips and Priestley (see Chapter 2), intended to inform the investor or general businessman, the first guides to the waterways were written for potential cruisers, not for commercial users. This may lead the 'serious' historian to undervalue the early guides, but they constitute, especially if a number are used, a contemporary record of navigational and other details not easily found elsewhere.

The first demand for cruising guides came from the generation of young men inspired by MacGregor and his Canoe Club. Perhaps the earliest is the the anonymous *The Oarsman's Guide to the Thames* (c1856 – Grade D), actually by Thomas Wood, with a second edition in 1857 which included other rivers as well. The honorary secretary of the Leander Club, perhaps conscious of the difficulty English oarsmen might have with his name (Patrick MacChombaich de Colquhoun), produced his *A Companion to the Oarsman's Guide* (D) anonymously in 1857 too, and these guides remained the best available until 1896. In that year, Francis Prothero and William Clark compiled an admirably researched and extensive *Cruising Club Manual. A New Oarsman's Guide to the Rivers and Canals of Great Britain and Ireland* (D), complete with a folding map contained in a pocket at the rear. A large number of waterways are included, many not navigable by anything more demanding than a canoe, but the authors explained that they had omitted 'any river or canal that passes wholly or in great part through a grimy manufacturing district' and, surprisingly, the Thames below

Oxford. The book is well laid out, and each waterway receives some general remarks, a table of distances, hints on navigation, and comments on the scenery. Nearly 200 waterways are thus described in detail, and because all the first-hand knowledge necessary to provide this detail could hardly have been acquired by the editors themselves, they made use of information from 'brother oarsmen in every part of the kingdom'. It is interesting to see that some of the canal information was supplied by Mr R.De Salis, cousin of Henry Rodolph De Salis, and author of *Thirty Days on English Canals, with some remarks on canal development* (D), published privately in 1894.

> '...thirty years of recurring summer vacations largely spent in cruising on inland waters have afforded me opportunities of exploring, in launch, canoe or rowboat - mainly the latter - all, or nearly all, of the rivers and canals of the kingdom, and the abounding pleasure derived therefrom has induced me to proffer such guidance as may herein be found for the behoof of fellow Aquatics.'

Thus George Westall introduces his *Inland Cruising on the Rivers and Canals of England and Wales* (1908 – Grade D). This follows the standard pattern for a cruising guide, with remarks and distance tables for each waterway, and a large folding map in three colours at the front. His coverage is not as good as that of Prothero and Clark – not only does he restrict himself to England and Wales, but also includes far fewer of the smaller rivers. His total of waterways is thus only about half that of the earlier guide. In fact, it is hard to see what gap Westall meant to fill, given the prior existence of both the *Cruising Club Manual* and Bradshaw's guide.

The first Bradshaw had appeared in 1904. Its full title is lengthy, but explanatory: *Bradshaw's Canals and Navigable Rivers of England and Wales. A Handbook of Inland Navigation for manufacturers, merchants, traders, and others: Compiled, after a Personal Survey of the whole of the Waterways, by Henry Rodolph De Salis, Assoc. M. Inst. C.E., Director: Fellows, Morton, & Clayton, Ltd., Canal Carriers.* De Salis came from a family long associated with canals and was keen to see their use increased. Realising that no commercial handbook was available containing 'the most ordinary information concerning places to which cargoes can be sent, and under what circumstances', he set out to provide such information. To collect it, he covered 14,000 miles in eleven years, much of it (but presumably not all) in his steam launch *Dragonfly*. The extent of these cruises may still be a record, certainly making

Bonthron look like the weekend boater he was. The book is a handsome one, with deep green cloth which carries its gilt well, but apart from the folding map, is devoid of any illustrations except those in the advertisements at the back. It ran to two further editions: 1918 and 1928, and all are Grade D. Copies are not particularly scarce, but are usually well worn. I presume that many first served their time in an office, and then went on to do duty afloat as cruising guides. Only late on life have they come to rest on the book-collectors' shelves, to be cherished at last, and that's really a pretty good record for any book.

With new and secondhand Bradshaws around for the next thirty years, there was no real need for any other guide. It is true that F.C.South compiled *The British and Irish Waterways Gazetteer* (D) in 1911, but its great rarity surely reflects limited sales on publication. The next important guide doesn't appear until 1939, when Imray, Laurie, Norie & Wilson published W.Eric Wilson's *Inland Waterways of Great Britain* (BC). Although useful, the book has two annoying features: the spine is completely blank, and folding map is not always provided with a pocket, but may be merely loosely dropped into the back. It therefore just as easily drops out, and many mapless copies exist. I know that the presence of a pocket doesn't guarantee the presence of a map, but it's a help, and I once had the pleasant surprise of finding a Bradshaw with two maps in its pocket! Wilson's book went into a second edition in 1947 (B) – the last guide to appear before the nationalisation of many of our waterways under the 1947 Transport Act. Nationalisation, and the foundation of the Inland Waterways Association in 1946, produced enough changes to merit another edition, but this time the same publishers produced Lewis Edwards' *Inland Waterways of Great Britain and Northern Ireland* (BC) in 1950.

This remains the standard work, and has been revised from time to time. The latest edition is the fifth (1972 – Grade B), and a new edition is currently in preparation. However, at some time between 1962 and 1972, the author chose to acknowledge positively the descent of his book from the earlier work by Wilson. Accordingly he called the third edition of his own book the 'Fifth', and the verso of its title page lists the 1950 edition as 'Third' and the 1962 edition as 'Fourth' – even though no copies were ever printed bearing those words. Thus do authors create puzzles for bibliographers. In addition, there has been continuous vacillation about Ireland. In 1950 Northern Ireland was included, in 1962 coverage extended to the whole of Ireland, but in 1972 it disappeared completely.

18

The British and Irish
Waterways Gazetteer.

Comprising a Directory of Steamship, Hoy and Canal Companies, together with a List of London Wharves and Licensed Lightermen ; also about seven thousand Water Routes to over two thousand important places in the United Kingdom.

Compiled, Classified and Arranged
——— — ——— by ———— —— ———
FREDERICK CHARLES SOUTH.

LONDON :
The Stanmer Publishing Company,
4 Kersley Street, Battersea, S.W.
1910.

Fifteenth Edition—Revised

SALTER'S GUIDE
TO THE
THAMES

" To thee, my silver footed Thamesis. "—R. Herrick.

AND TO
The Rivers Avon, Severn, and Wye,
and the Principal Canals

BY

J. H. SALTER & J. A. SALTER.

Oxford :
ALDEN & Co., LTD., 35, CORN-MARKET STREET,
LONDON :
SIMPKIN, MARSHALL, HAMILTON, KENT AND CO., LTD.
[ENTERED AT STATIONERS' HALL.]

A commercial guide of 1910,
and a pleasure guide of 1912.

Not every boater wants to travel the whole waterway system (not at first, that is; the malady takes some time to develop), so there is a place for the local guide, covering one waterway or area. Guides to the Thames abound, and we have already seen how the earliest national guides grew from those for the Thames. On the Broads, the development of a major boating industry in the last century made the production of a cheap and reliable guide an essential. The most succesful of these was *The Handbook to the Rivers & Broads of Norfolk & Suffolk* (BC), by George Christopher Davies. The first edition is dated 1882, and the latest I have come across is the 50th, dated 1929. Somewhere along the line, the first three words were dropped from the title, but the style remains essentially unaltered. A collection of a dozen editions spanning the years would be most interesting and attractive, showing a variety of pictorial cloth covers and text illustrations. Ernest Suffling also did quite well with his *The Land of the Broads. A practical guide for yachtsmen...* (1887 – Grade BC) which ran to at least seven editions, some of them illustrated. When Broads cruising became less fashionable, though no less popular, it was the boat companies themselves who wrote and sold the guides. Thus in 1926 we find Leo Robinson, with a large hire fleet and a boatyard, writing and publishing *Yachting on the Broads* (B), which survived until well after the war, its 12th edition being dated 1953. Later Broads cruising literature is unremarkable, although David & Charles did include a volume on the Broads in their 'Holiday Cruising' series – *Holiday Cruising on the Broads and Fens* (1972 – Grade A) by Lewis Edwards.

On the Thames, much the same pattern occurs, with many fine books on the river and its valley dating from the eighteenth and nineteenth centuries, a wealth of cruising guides from the fashionable days, and then a decline into boatyard publications. That great Thames photographer, Henry Taunt, produced a number of guides and picture-books on the Thames in the second half of the last century, and John Salter, of the well-known Oxford boatyard, first published his *Guide to the River Thames* (B) in about 1883. The 57th edition appeared in about 1960, although bearing no resemblance to the original, and it may still be in print. Again repeating Broads history, David & Charles published *Holiday Cruising on the Thames* (A) by E. and P.Ball in 1970.

The Transport Act of 1947 created the largest waterway authority ever seen in Britain – the Docks & Inland Waterways Executive of the British Transport Commission, which took over some 2,000 miles of rivers and canals. Some of these had been independent, some railway-owned, and two (the Caledonian and Crinan Canals) had been controlled by the Ministry of Transport since 1919. Although there wasn't at first much pleasure cruising, DIWE was keen to encourage its growth, and it soon became clear that only cruising could offer any future at all for a number of waterways, even though revenue from recreation would be unlikely to cover maintenance costs. Accordingly, in 1956 British Transport Waterways (successor to DIWE) launched its series of 'Inland Cruising Booklets' (individually A, with a full set Grade D). Number 1 was devoted to the Llangollen Canal, and was the first of a set of 16, each dealing with a single stretch of waterway, or a small group of connected waterways. Attractively produced, with photos, wood engravings and strip maps (initially printed in brown, later changed to blue), these were useful little guides, which remained the cruisers' staple for many years. Edwards was invaluable as a general reference, but not the book you took on board. The new guides showed the facilities, as well as the locks and bridges, although I must admit to cursing the publishers when more than once searching for pubs marked in a booklet, but which had long since vanished. They were, nevertheless, cheap and useful, and were revised in an *ad hoc* way from time to time. I remember the dismay with which the decision to phase these out was greeted – they were to be replaced with a series of four regional guides, each costing several times as much as one of our beloved booklets. The first of these *Nicholson's Guides to the Waterways* appeared in about 1971, and despite their price, they did prove useful. A good feature was the use of Ordnance Survey map originals to create a much more informative strip map; a missed opportunity was that British Waterways Board involvement limited coverage to BWB waterways, something one would have hoped could have been overcome, particularly as a Nicholson's Thames guide had been published in 1969. The canals of the Midlands were split between the four volumes, and so a fifth guide, covering the Midlands at a reduced scale, was published later. The next generation of *Nicholson's Guides* represented a distinct deterioration of standards, particularly on the maps, which shrank from 2 inches to the mile (enlarged from OS map) to 1 inch to 2 miles (redrawn, omitting much detail). The defects of this edition account for the high prices obtaining for the earliest edition (well up Grade A) and for Nicholson's decision to publish a new 2 inches to the mile edition in 1983.

Supplementing the limited coverage offered by BWB and Nicholson, there have been numerous local guides produced by a variety of bodies. For instance, the *River Wey and Godalming Navigations* was published by the IWA in 1969, the *Bridgewater Canal Guide* by the Manchester Ship Canal in about 1973, and *The Caldon Canal* (with a foreword by Tom Rolt) by the Caldon Canal Society in 1969. Many of these local guides are very useful, containing information not available elsewhere, but are rather elusive, sliding in and out of print without the benefit of national marketing. It is this, not their price (Grade A), which would make a comprehensive collection (or even a list of titles) difficult to assemble. Such a collection, however, could prove invaluable, as it is just this sort of material which slips through the net of the net of the Copyright Acts, and is thus poorly represented in national collections. If nothing else, perhaps I could exhort the publishers of these and similar booklets to send one copy of each to the British Library. This is, incidentally, a legal requirement anyway, under the Copyright Act 1911 (amended by the British Library Act 1972) but I make the plea on behalf of future historians and bibliographers, rather than out of any wish to see obedience to a regulation for its own sake.

Chapter 2

HISTORIES AND ENGINEERING

Cruising may well provide the initial interest, but the enquiring mind cannot long survive on a diet of cruising guides alone. Sooner or later, curiosity will throw up questions to which the cruising literature can provide only the sketchiest and most unreliable answers. Who built the canals, and when? When did the last commercial boats pass this way? Why was this particular route chosen? How were tunnels driven two hundred years ago? What was life like on the canals of the last century?

Histories

Without doubt, the best single general historical book is Charles Hadfield's *British Canals: an illustrated history*, the seventh edition of which was published in 1984 by David & Charles (yes, it's the same Charles). It has itself a long and distinguished history, as the first edition appeared in 1950, and it has been in print ever since, steadily undergoing revision, extension and improvement. The first edition (Grade B) is quite easily found, but not so often with its dustwrapper, which has a good photo, not included in the book itself, of a narrow-boat crossing Wolverton aqueduct. Some editions were produced in both hardback and paperback versions, and the first was reprinted by the Readers' Union in 1952, so it exists in about a dozen varieties, not counting at least two editions published in New York. There are traps for the bibliographer; the 1966 edition is described on the title page as the third impression of the second edition, but a few pages later we find the author's 'Preface to third edition'. Again, it wasn't until after some of the fourth edition paperbacks had been distributed that somebody realised that no new preface had been included, although it had been listed in the 'Contents.'

A particularly important feature of Hadfield's *British Canals* is that it is the pinnacle of a three-tiered pyramid of waterway books published by David & Charles. The second tier is the *Canals of the British Isles* series comprising twelve titles, two of which are in two volumes. Most were written in whole or in part by Charles Hadfield, and the series was of course produced under his direction. The titles are *The Canals of*

Eastern England, of *the East Midlands*, of *the North of Ireland*, of *North West England* (2 vols), *of Scotland*, of *the South of Ireland*, of *South and South East England*, of *South Wales and the Border*, of *South West England*, of *the West Midlands*, of *Yorkshire and North East England* (2 vols) and, finally, the odd man out, *Waterways to Stratford*. Not only is its title odd, but it also has a substantial portion devoted to the history of the Stratford & Moreton Tramway. A number have been revised, and some are still in print; all are Grade B except the two-volume works and *Canals of the South of Ireland* which are Grade C. The diligent may come across a volume of similar style, called *The Canals of Southern England* (1955 – Grade B) and wonder where it fits into the series. The answer is that it doesn't any more, having been replaced by the two separate volumes covering this area. A master index of all waterways in the British Isles is to be found in the later editions of *British Canals*, which directs the reader to the required volume in the series.

The bottom tier in the pyramid is the 'Inland Waterways Histories' series, each volume devoted to a single waterway or locality. Unlike the top two tiers, the coverage of this bottom tier is only patchy, as the majority of our waterways don't deserve a full-length book. Extra gaps exist because a number of titles were announced but never published. It is therefore worth listing the series in full: *The Ballinamore & Ballyconnell Canal* (by Patrick Flanagan), *The Birmingham Canal Navigations Volume 1: 1768-1846* (S.R.Broadbridge), *The Bude Canal* (Helen Harris and Monica Ellis), *The Dorset & Somerset Canal* (Kenneth R.Clew), *The Grand Canal of Ireland* (Ruth Delany), *The Grand Junction Canal* (Alan H.Faulkner), *The Grand Western Canal* (Helen Harris), *The Great Ouse* (Dorothy Summers), *The Kennet & Avon Canal* (Clew), *The Leicester Line* (Philip A.Stevens), *London's Lost Route to Basingstoke* (P.A.L.Vine), *London's Lost Route to the Sea* (Vine), *The Nutbrook Canal* (Peter Stevenson), *The Oxford Canal* (Hugh J.Compton), *The Royal Military Canal* (Vine), *The Somersetshire Coal Canal and Railways* (Clew), *The Thames & Severn Canal* (Humphrey Household), *The Trent & Mersey Canal* (Jean Lindsay), and *The Yorkshire Ouse* (Baron F.Duckham). This last title was in fact published first, and its success suggested to David & Charles that a series would be worthwhile. Some of the titles in the series have gone to two or three editions, and at least two were issued as paperbacks. Despite a number of the series having been remaindered, and some still being in print, a full set of 19 titles is not easily built up, but a line-up of good copies in dustwrapper makes a fine sight. Most elusive are *The Thames & Severn* (C), *Basingstoke* (D), *Grand Junction* (C) and Duckham's *Ouse* (C); the rest are Grade B except for *The Great Ouse, Grand Canal of Ireland* and *Ballinamore & Ballyconnell,* which are Grade A. Ironically, the Ballinamore & Ballyconnell Canal itself seems only to have been used by 15 boats; a century later it seems that the book was only bought by 15 people, as remainder bookshops had it piled waist-high for years. Not that there was anything particularly wrong with either canal or book, except that neither appears to have answered a real need!

There are, of course, other modern books providing both general and particular canal history. L.T.C.Rolt's *The Inland Waterways of England* (BC) and Eric de Maré's *The Canals of England* (CD) were published in 1950, the year of the first edition of *British Canals.* As this was also the year in which John O'Connor's *Canals, Barges and People* (CD) appeared, we can look on 1950 as the dawn of the new Canal Age in publishing, for there has been a growing flow of canal books ever since. Rolt's book provides a general view of its subject, and is a very readable introduction to waterway history, although lacking the precision and detail of Hadfield. By 1970, it had gone through five impressions, with some small changes; in 1979 a second edition was produced, but one scarcely different from the first except that it carries a foreword by Charles Hadfield. De Maré's book has more immediate appeal than the other two, being a quarto volume, with 177 illustrations, most of which are photographs. In word and picture, it succeeds in conveying the flavour of canals and the canalside scene, making no pretence to be a comprehensive text. It, too, has been reissued with minor revisions, the fourth impression being dated 1965. Its evocative qualities are still recognised, and it remains in short supply. Since 1950, many publishers have added general canal books to their lists, but most have been undistinguished compared with these first three. Perhaps the best two are Hugh McKnight's *The Shell Book of Inland Waterways* (1975 – Grade B; 2nd edition 1981) and Edward Paget-Tomlinson's *The Complete Book of Canal & River Navigations* (1978 – Grade C). It's not actually complete, but it is certainly very comprehensive, and contains some finely printed colour plates of C.V.Wain's careful drawings of working boats. It is also physically a large book, having 361 A4 pages. It is, however, sad that such a well researched book has had to be printed from typescript, and lacks an index. Finally, although not a history, the *Waterways Atlas of the British Isles* (1966 – Grade BC) by

John Cranfield and Michael Bonfiel is a very useful reference for the historian.

In this section, I have started from the modern end, for the very good reason that, on the whole, modern historical books are better than older ones. The modern author has at his disposal for more information, better libraries, better printing and illustrating techniques, and the work of other writers to build on. This doesn't reduce the problems of writing a *good* book, but it does put today's writer in a very good starting position. Having looked at the post-war literature first therefore, let us now leap backwards to the eighteenth century, and start again in the middle of the canal age itself.

The first book calling itself a waterway history was published in 1766, under the title *The History of Inland Navigations. Particularly those of the Duke of Bridgewater...* (GH). No author is named, and the Bridgewater connection must have suggested to some long-dead bookseller that the book was by James Brindley. This myth is almost as widely believed as the other myth about Brindley – that he was illiterate. He was certainly not illiterate, as his surviving diaries and notebooks show, but almost certainly he was not the author of *The History of Inland Navigations*.

Numerous books have been devoted to our rivers, either individually or collectively, but the majority are general topographical and historical works, in which accounts of towns, churches, and country seats receive far more space than do the navigations. However, the spreading of inland navigation throughout the greater part of England, Wales and lowland Scotland in the few decades following 1760 produced a need for a general reference book for waterway users and investors. Three authors looked to fill this gap – John Cary, John Phillips and Joseph Priestley. Phillips was the most successful of the three; his *General History of Inland Navigation, Foreign and Domestic, containing a complete account of the canals already executed in England...* first appeared in 1792 (Grade G). It is a handsome quarto volume, with a fine folding map, and provides a good general account of canal development throughout the world, and then a lot of detail on individual 'domestic' navigations. Second and third quarto editions followed in 1793 and 1795 (both Grade G) but by 1803 it was reduced to an unremarkable, if fat, octavo volume without a map (Grade C). The fifth and last edition (Grade E) was undated, but was in fact published in 1809, and its text is identical to that of the fourth edition. Variant copies of the fourth and fifth editions exist, but these variations only extend to the title page. For

A

GENERAL HISTORY

OF

INLAND NAVIGATION,

Foreign and Domestic:

CONTAINING

A COMPLETE ACCOUNT OF THE CANALS

ALREADY EXECUTED IN

ENGLAND;

WITH

CONSIDERATIONS ON THOSE PROJECTED.

▬▬▬

BY J. PHILLIPS,

AUTHOR OF THE NEW BUILDERS PRICE BOOK.

▬▬▬

THE FIFTH EDITION.

▬▬▬▬▬▬

London:

PRINTED FOR B. CROSBY AND CO.

Stationers' Court, Paternoster Row;

Heather, Leadenhall-Street; Reddish, Manchester; Heaton, Leeds; Wright and **Co.**
Willan, and John Jones, Liverpool; Hartley, Rochdale, Holden, Halifax; Walker,
Chester; Akenhead, Newcastle upon Tyne; Booth, Norwich; Richardson, Bristol;
Jackson, Louth; Rooe, and Drakard, Stamford; Munday, Oxford; Ferraby, Hull;
Curson, Exeter; Robinson, and Sutton, Nottingham; Wilkins, Derby; Hall,
Worcester; Rollason, Coventry; Ellerby, Boston; Mottley and Co. and
Mc'Donald, Portsmouth; Horsey, Portsea; and Townson, Chatham.

1089.

One of the variant title-pages of Phillips' *General History*.

example, one of the fourth edition issues has a title page in which the author describes himself as 'sometime surveyor to the canals in Russia', and a fifth edition issue˙ exists with the date '1089'. This provides a possible clue to the reason why most copies of the fifth edition are undated; one can guess that when the type was originally set up, a mistake was made in the date. A few copies were run off before the error was spotted, and the offending type removed. Then, by accident or design, it was never replaced, and the vast majority have no date, Norman or otherwise. It is impossible to date the book from internal evidence, which in part explains why the David & Charles facsimile (Grade C) of the fifth edition is dated 1805. Curiosities apart, the third edition is probably the most desirable, being the most informative of the three quarto editions.

Cary aimed to provide much more detailed topographical information on canals than could be included in Phillips' single map and, as befits a London engraver and mapseller, he made the finely engraved maps the main feature of his *Inland Navigation*, subtitled *Select Plans of the Several navigable canals, throughout Great Britain...*, dated 1795. It appeared, in fact, in four distinct parts: 1795, 1796, 1798 and 1808. Each part contains 4 folding maps, and accompanying text. The quality of the maps has ensured that quite a few have survived, but the intervals between publication have militated against their survival in complete sets. Individual maps would be Grade D, a whole set Grade G. Well after the flowering of the canal age, Priestley produced his useful and sober *Historical Account of the navigable rivers, canals and railways, throughout Great Britain...* in 1831 (F). This was intended as a supporting text to a large canal map by Nicholls, Priestley & Walker. The original edition is quarto, with the preface dated October 1st, 1830. Its worth has already been assessed by Charles Hadfield:

> 'In the days before the penny post, the telephone or the typewriter, he managed to compile an almost complete list of canal and railway Acts and, using them as a basis, to write a short account of each line, full of useful information and without padding, the sort of book that would have been invaluable to canal officials and traders, investors, members of Parliament, land-owners and business men generally. That it is still so useful to students a century and a quarter later is a measure of its value.'

Later, in 1831, an octavo edition appeared (Grade F). This has an identical preface, dated April 1831, but the text had been entirely reset, and some of the entries re-ordered. It is thus quite clearly a distinct edition, and it is not correct to describe the two editions as 'large paper' and 'small paper', which would imply printing from the same type. Perhaps uniquely, both editions have been reproduced in facsimile. In 1967, Cass published a facsimile (Grade D) of the quarto edition, misleadingly calling their printing the 'Second edition'. Two years later, David & Charles reprinted the octavo edition (Grade C) on the grounds that its text incorporates all the material contained in the appendix and corrigendum to the quarto edition, and that the smaller paper size makes it a handier volume.

The rapid rise of the railways diverted attention, funds and trade from the canals, and many years went by before any more general works were attempted. Towards the end of the century, there was some disaffection with the near monopoly of the railways, and some traders cast envious eyes across the Channel, where waterway systems had not suffered the same neglect, and were still able to offer real competition to rail. In the 1880s and 1890s, a new optimism arose, the most obvious fruits of which were the construction of the Manchester Ship Canal, and the (later) establishment of a Royal Commission to study the waterways of the British Isles and make recommendations for their future. Indicative of the rising interest are *Waterways and Water Transport in Different Countries* (D) by J.S.Jeans (1890) and the slimmer and less well-known *The Canal System of England* (C) by H.G.Thompson (1902). The Royal Commission proved a paragon of thoroughness, producing no less than 12 foolscap volumes between 1906 and 1911. Complete sets of these are exceedingly rare, though odd volumes creep onto the market occasionally at Grade BC, and a patient man might seek to build up a set piecemeal.

The Royal Commission's recommendations were not, alas, adopted; had they been, the waterway system of England would certainly now look very different. It is tempting to attribute at least some of this neglect to the energy of Edwin Pratt, a staunch supporter of railways, who conducted a vigorous campaign against any State involvement in waterways. First came *Railways and their Rates, with an appendix on the British Canal Problem* (1905); this was followed by *British Canals: is their resuscitation practicable?* (1906) and *Canals and Traders: the argument pictorial as applied to the report of the Royal Commission on Canals and Waterways* (1910). All are Grade C, although the paperback edition of the first could be B. From their titles alone, their viewpoint is clear, and it is certainly a viewpoint which won the day. None of the three is particularly scarce, which presumably reflects largish print runs, in turn suggesting considerable influence. The same cannot be said of his

28

much later *Scottish Canals and Waterways* (1922 – Grade D), occasioned by a desire to thwart further public investment in Scotland's canals and, in particular, in any scheme for a ship canal between the Forth and the Clyde, an idea then receiving considerable public interest.

Although there is no doubt of the partisan nature of Pratt's approach, his works are based on a great deal of research, and are therefore useful if read with care. To him, indeed, must go the crown for the earliest general history of transport, his *History of Inland Transport and Communication* (C) appearing in 1912. This represents the first attempt to study the development of transport as a whole, with all the complex interactions between the different modes, and between them and other industries. It is not particularly rare, and its availability has been much increased by its being reprinted in facsimile by David & Charles in 1970 (C). Only a few more years passed before a far more scholarly work on the same subject was published by Cambridge University Press: W.T.Jackman's *The Development of Transportation in Modern England* (1916 – Grade DE), whose two volumes present a finely detailed and referenced account, followed by a bibliography occupying over 60 pages. One can only regret that his interpretation of the word 'modern' was a little restricted; his history goes little farther than 1850, whereas Pratt, despite publishing earlier, takes us up to 1911. The original edition of Jackman is rare, and although Cass have printed two facsimile editions (both CD), these are not easily found.

The Royal Commission and its deliberations created a general interest which was reflected in a number of books discussing the future of waterways, published during the first two decades of the century. A useful and thorough survey is contained in *Our Waterways: a history of inland navigation considered as a branch of water conservancy* (1906 – Grade D) by U.A.Forbes and W.H.R.Ashford, and the same year saw the publication of a paper which had been given at the Institution of Civil Engineers in November 1905 by John Saner. Saner had been the Engineer to the Weaver Navigation since 1888, and was very active in promoting modern waterway transport. While preparing his paper, *On Waterways in Great Britain* (C), he wrote to 63 navigation companies, most of whom replied, and he then collated their information into a series of detailed tables describing the leading features of each, including sizes, engineering aspects, water supply, trading position and so on, distinguishing between the independent and the railway owned lines. Thus his paper provides a useful survey of waterways in the British Isles, just before the Royal Commission's own report. When the latter was published, a flurry of interest was provoked, and amongst its results was J.S.Nettlefold's charming, if hopelessly optimistic, *Garden Cities and Canals* (1914 – Grade C), a vision born of Ebenezer Howard out of Royal Commission. We even find, during this period, that not all the railway writers shared Pratt's views; in 1916 Roy Horniman, in his *How to Make the Railways Pay for the War* (B), argued not only for wholesale reorganisation of the railways, but also that the way in whch rail and water competition had been stifled was not in the national interest. He even produced data to show that in many cases barges actually provided higher overall journey speeds than trains, the latter being hampered by disproportionate delays at the terminals and marshalling yards, and finally wished to see waterways improved to take bulk goods unsuited to railways.

After the first World War, the literature thins out. Several good books did appear in the next twenty years, including the businesslike *Canals and Inland Waterways* (1929 – Grade CD) by George Cadbury (then Chairman of the Severn & Canal Carrying Co., and Managing Director of Cadbury Brothers) and S.P.Dobbs. This deserves to be more widely known, if only for its unusual photos of whole railway coaches being barged down the Trent. An outstanding contribution to earlier history was made by T.S.Willan with his *River Navigation in England 1600-1750* (1936 – Grade D), whose excellently devised and researched maps of England's navigable rivers at three different dates have been much reproduced by later writers. The first edition is scarce, but the quality of Willan's work made a facsimile possible, and this was published by Cass in 1964 (C).

This brings us virtually to our 1950 starting point, but mention should be made of a few of the more important monographs. In terms of quality of publication, printing and sheer size, those on the Manchester Ship Canal and the Ribble Navigation are easy winners. Naturally the former stimulated a lot of writing from well before its start, right through its construction, and after its opening in 1894. John Heywood, a local Manchester printer and publisher, produced numerous guides and picture books for local sale. However, civic pride demanded a written record matching the canal in scale and grandeur, and this was published in 1907. Sir Bosdin Leech's *History of the Manchester Ship Canal* (F) is a handsome work, in two quarto volumes, with many photos and folding plates. Unfortunately, it has a few folding plans in pockets at the rear of each volume, and this is a recipe for uncompleteness, but it remains the grandest of all Britain's navigation histories. Civic pride also fired its nearest rival – James Barron's *A History of the Ribble Navigation* (D), published for the Corporation of Preston in 1938. Preston Dock, at 40 acres the country's largest dock when built, has recently been closed to commercial traffic, but will probably be preserved as a marina. Barron's fine quarto volume, profusely illustrated, provides a useful history of both the navigation and the dock.

Other notable monographs include David Tew's *Oakham Canal* (E) published in a limited edition of 450 by the Brewhouse Press in 1968, and illustrated by Rigby Graham. Not surprisingly, it is difficult to acquire, although I must express my own grumble that any book about a canal should, as a *sine qua non*, have a map! Fred Thacker, legendary Thames-lover, produced two very detailed books on the Thames at his own expense: *The Thames Highway: a history of the inland navigation* (1914 – Grade D) and *The Thames Highway: a history of the locks and weirs* (1920 – Grade D). They constitute a valuable history, culled from many primary sources (and thus immediately distinguished from the majority of Thames books), and their quality fully justifies their re-issue in facsimile (CD for the pair) by David & Charles in 1968. It is, of course, not possible to list all navigation histories here, but the foregoing will, I hope, provide some idea of the variety of books which exists.

Engineering

Much of the early hydraulic engineering advice rests on texts which originated from mainland Europe. The most widely used of these would be Belidor's *Architecture Hydraulique* (first published in 4 volumes 1737-1753) which provides a well-illustrated account of contemporary hydraulic engineering, including, of course, waterways. Many editions were produced, but all are Grade G or above. Less widely known is Paolo Frisi's *Treatise on rivers and torrents... to which is added an essay on navigable canals*, first published in Italy in 1762, but highly enough valued in Britain to be published (in translation) several times during the next hundred years, first as a handsome quarto in 1818 (F), and last as a humble octavo in Weale's Rudimentary Series (C) in about 1872.

Encyclopaedias also provide useful information, that of Abraham Rees (1819) proving a particularly rich quarry for later writers. Edward Cresy published his comprehensive *Encyclopaedia of civil engineering* in 1847, and this contains a broad review of all branches of civil engineering, with an extensive historical survey covering foreign as well as British work. It was produced in two volumes (sometimes bound as

one or three), and contains over 3,000 wood engravings. The eighth
edition of *Encyclopaedia Britannica* contained an entry 'Inland
Navigation' by David Stevenson, which was reprinted as a separate book
Canal and river engineering (1858), and this itself went into two further
editions under the new title *Principles and practice of canal and river
engineering* (1872 and 1886). All three editions are scarce, and Grade D.

One of Britain's earliest books devoted to canal engineering alone is
Robert Fulton's *Treatise on the Improvement of Canal Navigation*
(1796 – Grade G). This attractive work has the added interest that its 17
plates were engraved by Fulton himself. It is, however, largely an
exposition of Fulton's ideas for building very small canals (for boats of 2
to 5 tons), rather than a record of canal engineering practice of the late
eighteenth century. Its most striking feature is Plate 13 – the first known
drawing of a cast iron aqueduct, and one which has much in common
with that later built at Pont Cysyllte. A much more sober canal engineer
was stimulated to produce a reply to Fulton; this was William Chapman
whose *Observations on the various systems of Canal navigation...in
which Mr Fulton's plan of wheel-boats and...small canals are
particularly investigated...* (1797 – Grade G) rather surprisingly ends
with an account of the canals and inclined planes in China.

One of Fulton's drawings of a cast-iron aqueduct, published in 1796.

The last major canal engineering book was that by L.F.Vernon-Harcourt; his *Treatise on Rivers and Canals* (E) was first published in two volumes in 1882, with all the text in the first, and the 21 folding plates in the second volume. The second edition (1896 – Grade E) was rewritten and rearranged, with the first volume being subtitled 'Rivers' and the second 'Canals'. British attitudes to canals this century have been such that no engineering text books have been necessary. Later books are disappointing; neither E.S.Bellasis in his *River and Canal Engineering* (1913 – Grade C), nor R.C.Minikin in *Practical River and Canal Engineering* (1920 – Grade C), provides more than the slightest introduction to the subject, and details must be sought either in engineering journals or in foreign books. An excellent example of the latter was published in 1927 in Berlin – *Verkehrswasserbau* by Otto Franzius. Fortunately all the chapters relating directly to navigation were translated by an American, and published by the Massachusetts Institute of Technology in 1936 as *Waterway Engineering* (CD).

From this point on, the books are historical rather than practical. No solid comprehensive account of the development of navigation engineering has yet been written. The best is perhaps Anthony Burton's *The Canal Builders* (2nd edn 1981) – not to be confused with a book of the same title by Robert Payne, published in New York in 1959, but reasonably common in this country (Grade B). Tom Rolt contributed the volume *Navigable Waterways* (1969 – Grade B) to the Longmans Industrial Archaeology series he was editing; this is more often found as the later paperback reprint by Arrow (1973 – Grade A). D.D.Gladwin and J.M.White included a volume *Engineers and Engineering* in their three-volume work *English Canals* (each A), but despite having put a lot of work into it, they only produced a sketchy account, and one whose reliability is much impaired by the presence of an unforgivably large number of errors of fact and proof-reading. Periodicals again provide high quality papers on certain aspects of the subject, and the indexes to the *Transactions of the Newcomen Society* and the *Journal of the Railway and Canal Historical Society* are useful starting points for anyone wishing to pursue research in this area.

Engineering biography

Engineering seems to have been regarded as a pretty lowly pursuit until 1861, when Samuel Smiles published the first of his three-volume work *Lives of the Engineers* (DE). The third volume came out in 1862, and there seem to have been several printings. For all its bias and faults, it is absolutely essential reading for anyone interested in the Industrial Revolution. Its subtitle, *...a history of inland communication in Britain*, gives some idea of its scope, which includes Brindley, Myddleton, Smeaton, Telford, Rennie and George and Robert Stephenson. It was well received, and was later reissued as a five-volume revised edition in 1874, and as a 'popular' edition in 1904 (both DE). The sequence of issues is complicated by the appearance of reprints in 1878 and 1879, and of single volumes in 1864, *James Brindley and the Early Engineers* (C), and 1867, *The Life of Thomas Telford* (C). Both are adapted from material already published in *Lives of the Engineers*. As the individual volumes in the five-volume sets were not numbered, but in fact were parts of a series, each of which could be bought and used independently, there are numerous opportunities for odd volumes and pairs to turn up without their brothers, or even in the company of older cousins. Such wandering specimens would be priced BC.

The Lives of the Engineers has had an influence on engineering biography and history which is so all-pervading that it is difficult, even today, to distinguish clearly between what happened, and what we perceive through Smiles' eye and pen. It is easy enough to discover which facts (or fictions) come from Smiles alone, but what is easy to forget is that our view of the relative importance of individual engineers is still not merely tinged, but indelibly stained, with Smiles' ideas, and we have to work hard to throw these off. Perhaps the most striking example is that of William Jessop, whom Smiles deals with in a mere half page (and his three volumes ran to 1500 pages in total). For a hundred years, the view that Jessop was a minor figure was barely challenged, until two of our leading engineering historians, Charles Hadfield and Professor Skempton, wrote *William Jessop, Engineer* (B) in 1979. They found not only that he had been such an important and prolific engineer that it proved impossible to do him full justice in their 300-page book, but also that he was *the* most important civil engineer in Britain for some twenty years from about 1785. Our debt to Smiles is great, but should be acknowledged with caution.

The only other writer to tackle engineering biography systematically, and to develop an approach to it which does justice to the technical aspects yet creates a story which appeals far beyond engineering historians, is Tom Rolt. Of his three great biographies, it is only *Thomas Telford* (BC) which concerns us here. First published in 1958, it has remained in print virtually continuously since then. Incidentally, amongst his shorter biographies, he wrote one on Jessop in his *Great Engineers* (AB), published in 1962.

Apart from these two major authors, there are a number of minor figures, some of whom have produced good work. Perhaps because of the obvious romance of great civil engineering works, often carried out by men of lowly origin, there have been as many biographies written for children as for adults, but these will not be considered here. A sound, albeit very brief, introduction was provided in 1942 by Metius Chappell in his *British Engineers* (B), one of the less common members of the 'Britain in Pictures' series. Telford wrote his own biography, published posthumously with John Rickman as editor in 1838. This takes the form of a fat quarto volume of text, dwarfed by a folio 'atlas' containing 82 engraved plates. (These are actually numbered 1-83, with no number 28). This disparity of size between the two parts means that they often get separated. Presumably there were originally equal numbers, but it is the atlas which appears to come on to the market more frequently, and this would be Grade GH. I have never seen the text sold separately, and almost any pair would be Grade H, probably over £1,000.

Telford has ever since been an easy target for the biographer, and several unremarkable biographies have been written since Smiles. A sound, but unexciting, example is Sir Alexander Gibb's *The story of Telford: the rise of civil engineering* (1935), which would be Grade C if in good condition with its dustwrapper. The Duke of Bridgewater has also attracted quite a lot of attention, and several biographies exist. These include Bernard Falk's *The Bridgewater Millions – a candid family history* (1942 – Grade B), Hugh Malet's *The Canal Duke* (1961 – Grade B) and this same author's *Bridgewater: the Canal Duke, 1736-1803* (1977 – Grade B). Brindley has not been so well served, although Cyril Boucher's claim in his *James Brindley* (1968 – Grade B) that previously Brindley 'has never been honoured with a single volume' is patently untrue, as it overlooks Laurence Meynell's *James Brindley: the Pioneer of Canals* (1956 – Grade B), and Stanley Buckley's *James Brindley* (1948 – Grade A) which may be slight, but is nonetheless real. An excellent case study, *Brindley at Wet Earth Colliery: an engineering study* (B) was written by A.G.Banks and R.B.Schofield, and published by David & Charles in 1968.

Robert Fulton has his biographer in Henry Dickinson, who wrote *Robert Fulton, engineer and artist; his life and works* in 1913. This is very scarce, and would be Grade D if you could catch up with it. The American facsimile edition of 1971 is Grade C.

Chapter 3

BOATS AND TRAFFIC

Boats and boatmen received little attention from the early writers. The former were considered too mundane to be worthy of more than a passing mention, and the latter would have probably escaped notice altogether had they not quickly acquired a reputation for a variety of vices, particularly those involving other people's property, and excessive drinking. Such early books as were written about boats are largely concerned with the methods of propulsion. Thus we find Thomas Grahame advocating the adoption of 'fly boats' of the Scottish type when writing his *Letter to the Traders and Carriers on the Navigations Connecting Liverpool and Manchester* (1833 – Grade D), and William Fairbairn arguing for steam propulsion in his *Remarks on Canal Navigation* (1831 – Grade DE). F.J.Meyer and W.Wernigh wrote *Steam Towing on Rivers and Canals* (1876 – Grade D) to generate interest in their patent system in which a steam tug hauled itself and a string of barges upstream against the fiercest currents by gripping a steel cable laid along the bed of the river. In an appendix, unfortunately loosely inserted in the book and therefore not always present, they reveal that they had patented a cable tug for English narrow canals, 60 feet in length and 7 feet in beam, capable of towing 800 tons. Although the principle has been applied to ferries in Britain, I do not know of any cable or chain tugs ever being used regularly on waterways in this country, apart from through Islington and Harecastle Tunnels, despite their wide adoption in Germany, France, Russia, Canada and the USA.

It was George Smith, ardent reforming philanthropist, who first drew attention to the boatmen rather than the boats. Son of a brickmaker, his first campaign was to improve the lot of children working in the brickyards, and his success on this front led to his dismissal from his job of colliery manager at Coalville. In 1873 he decided to devote his life to the 'boat people' – i.e. the canal boatmen and their families. He wrote numerous letters and articles on this subject, and his book *Our Canal Population: the sad condition of the women and children – with remedy* (CD) appeared in 1875, with a new edition under the more appealing subtitle *a cry from the boat cabins, with remedy* in about 1879. This later edition was reprinted in facsimile in 1974 (B), but copies of all three printings are difficult to find. We can attribute the passing of the Canal Boats Act of 1877 to Smith's efforts, although it failed to achieve his aims. His campaign continued with *Canal Adventures by Moonlight* (1881 – Grade C) which describes some of Smith's personal encounters with boatmen, and also reprints many of Smith's letters to the papers.

Smith ploughed a lonely furrow and, after his death in 1895, no champion arose to continue his work. Quiet set on the canal scene, in a literary sense at least, until after the second World War. In 1942 the Grand Union Canal Company started to train girls 'off the land' to crew narrow boats, as there were insufficient experienced boaters to handle all the traffic available. Clearly, girls attracted by the idea would have been out of the ordinary, so perhaps it is not surprising that, from the comparatively small number of trainees, three books arose. Susan Woolfitt was first off the mark with *Idle Women* (1947 – Grade D), followed closely by Emma Smith with *Maidens' Trip* in 1948. *Idle Women* may now fairly be called rare, never having been reprinted, but Smith's book exists in at least eight issues. The first edition (C) was published by Putnam in 1948, and the same type used for the 2nd impression in 1949, but labels with the name of McGibbon & Kee were pasted over the Putnam imprint at the foot of the title-page. A paperback was published next year by Pocket Books (AB) but that was the last of the ordinary unabridged editions. The book then seems to have been branded by publishers as a 'juvenile' (a non-derogatory term for a children's book), as the next four issues were all abridged for children by the author. Chatto & Windus included it in their Queen's Classics series in 1953, reprinted in 1957 and 1961, and Penguin published it as a Peacock in 1964, with a charming cover, considerably superior to both the dustwrapper of the original edition and the cover of the Pocket Book edition. It made a final appearance, unabridged, in a large-print edition published by Chivers in 1977.

Last of the three books to describe the GUCC training scheme was by the woman who actually did the training. Kit Gayford had started boating in 1941, and built up some experience before joining the GUCC, so her book *The Amateur Boatwomen* (AB), not published until 1973, has a broader coverage than the other two. Despite having been remaindered, this is now not a common book, and one which is rightly valued for its descriptions of life on the cut by a participant. One can say the same for Tim Wilkinson's *Hold on a Minute* (1965 – Grade B), which provides an excellent account of working on the GUC in the post-war years, certainly deserving of its reprints in paperback form in 1970 and 1977 (both B).

In recent years the working canal boat has come to be an object for study, rather than for experiencing, and there are a number of excellent works tackling the subject in detail. A.J.Lewery's *Narrow Boat Painting* (1974 – Grade B), Harry Hanson's *The Canal Boatmen 1760-1914* (1975 – Grade B) and *Canal People* (1978 – Grade B), D.J.Smith's *Canal Boats and Boaters* (1973 – Grade B) and Tom Chaplin's *The Narrow Boat Book* (1978 – Grade B) are all full-length books containing the fruits of a great deal of research. Even the boat horse now has been given the treatment in Donald Smith's *The Horse on the Cut* (1982). Amongst the smaller books and booklets, mention must be made of Tom Chaplin's *The Short History of the Narrowboat* (first appearing in 1967 and subsequently in various revised editions), Avril Lansdell's *The Clothes of Cut* (1975), and the excellent Robert Wilson series with titles such as *The Number Ones, Boatyards and Boatbuilding, Claytons of Oldbury, Mersey and Weaver Flats,* and *Roses and Castles.* All contain useful information not easily found elsewhere (if at all), and are good value at the lower end of Grade A. For Ireland, turn to *Portrait of the Grand Canal* (1969 – Grade A) by Gerard D'Arcy, the most useful sections of which describe that canal's boats and boatmen.

The Thames sailing barge acquired devotees rather earlier than did the canal boats proper and, because many barges were worked on the waterways of the South East, deserves a brief mention here. Frank Carr's *Sailing Barges* (CD) dates from 1931 (revised edition 1951, reprinted 1971) and E.G.Martin's *Sailorman* (BC) from 1933, and the immediate post-war years saw a number of books recording what was then obviously a doomed way of life. Thus we find Edgar March's *Spritsail Barges of the Thames and Medway* (1948 – Grade CD, and

1. Centre   2. Heart   3. Petals.   4. Leaves and flourishes.

Painting a daisy – from D.J.Smith's *Canal Boats and Boaters.*

reprinted in 1970), Arthur Bennett's *Tide Time* (1949 – Grade B), and Hervey Benham's *Last Stronghold of Sail* (1948 – Grade B). It is apposite to draw this list to a close with a barge-captain's own record of the last sailing barge to trade: *Last of the Sailormen* (1960 – Grade B) by Bob Roberts.

The Norfolk wherry has not inspired such strong affection, but George Green did write *The Norfolk Wherry: its construction, evolution and history* in 1937. At least I take it he did – I've never tracked down a copy, although I have seen the revised edition which appeared in 1953. Robert Malster's *Wherries and Waterways* (1971 – Grade AB) is an excellent study, well illustrated and presented. Another such is Roy Clark's *Black-sailed Traders* (1961 – Grade B) which also contains a long list of all the wherries known to the author. A recent little book which provides an excellent introduction to the subject is *The Sailing Barges of the Maritime England* (1982 – Grade A) by Tony Ellis, who includes information on barges from estuaries and rivers all round the country.

Unlike railways, canals have not stimulated a flood of picture books. This reflects both the fact that the camera did not become widely used until well after the railways had eclipsed the canals, and (I hope) the way in which canal enthusiasts perceive their subject. Nevertheless, a handful of picture books have emerged, most with an emphasis on craft, and very fascinating they are. De Maré's *The Canals of England* (1950 – Grade C) could perhaps be described as the first, but I feel that its text is too important for the book to be thought of as primarily pictorial. However, Hugh McKnight's *Canal and River Craft in Pictures* (1969 – Grade C) is unashamedly pictorial, with the text virtually limited to extended captions. I remember the joy with which I and my friends greeted its publication, and the hours we spent studying it. Pictorial books have the great virtue of including a wealth of incidental material, whether the 'author' would or no, and we combed the photos to glean shreds of authentic narrow boat detail. Copies are now hard to find, and the same is true of John Gagg's two pictorial books, published (rather surprisingly) by Ian Allan. These are *Canals in Camera* (1970 – Grade B) and *Canals in Camera – 2* (1971 – Grade B). For me, their interest is limited, as they contain only contemporary photos, all taken by the author on his extensive cruises.

Most of the later picture books are still fairly easily available. These include a number from Moorland Publishing, in their 'Historic Waterways Scenes' series, such as Peter Lead's *The Trent & Mersey*

Canal (1980) and Michael Ware's *Britain's Lost Waterways* (1979) in two volumes; all are Grade B.

Company Publications

Early canal companies did publish handbills, posters and other advertising and commercial matter, but these are too rare and varied to be worth describing here in any detail. It is really only the twentieth-century material which is likely to be found outside established collections, but these same collections may well be very weak on this later material. Almost none of the canal company handbooks, for instance, are to be found in the British Library.

Many of the companies produced quite elaborate and well illustrated handbooks to publicise their waterways. These are often hard to date without some knowledge of the company's history, but nevertheless offer valuable material for the historian. Typical of these are *The Aire & Calder Navigation: the water route between Lancashire & Yorkshire and the East Coast* (c.1923 – Grade BC), *The Calder & Hebble Navigation: general information...* (c.1937 – Grade BC), and *The Trent: a highway of commerce between the ports on the Humber and the industrial centres of the Midlands* (c.1938 – Grade B). Hardly snappy titles, but definitely worth reading. The Manchester Ship Canal also, of course, produced a great wealth of literature, and at one time supported a monthly magazine *Port of Manchester Official Sailing List & Shipping Guide*. The historian might also remember that handbooks for ports served by inland waterways (e.g. Bristol, Hull, London) can often provide good information, in text and in advert, about local waterways and the carriers working on them.

A particularly interesting pair of handbooks was produced by the Grand Union Canal Company in about 1935. *Arteries of Commerce* and *Making Transport History* (both D) have very similar contents, but were produced by two different commercial printers. These are amongst the most lavish of the handbooks, being quarto, and having 120 pages containing many maps, photos and adverts. These handbooks reflect the modern approach adopted by the Grand Union Canal Company, which was after all only founded in 1929. They also produced some finely printed maps (C) in this period, nominally of the connections with their own waterways, but virtually covering the whole of England. At 35 by 27 inches, and printed in six colours, these maps are decorative as well as useful, and serve as a reminder of the commercial confidence of the GUCC.

Chapter 4

OFFICIAL PUBLICATIONS

From time to time, various Government and Parliamentary Committees have reported on certain aspects of waterways and their management. Although at first it was assumed that the canal companies could go their own way, as legitimate expressions of free enterprise, the development of the enormous power of the railways in the last century at least raised the question as to whether the canals were being operated in the best interest, not of the companies themselves, but of the nation as a whole. In order to attempt an answer to such an almost unanswerable question, the first step is to find out what is actually going on. Thus we see in 1870, the House of Commons commissioning *A return from all the inland navigation and canal companies in England and Wales* (D) containing, amongst other things, the dividends paid to shareholders, and the tonnages conveyed for 1828, 1838, 1848, 1858, and 1868. Typical of such publications, it consists of nearly 200 closely printed foolscap pages, passing dull to look upon, but packed with interest for the historian, as it represents the first attempt to produce national carrying figures for the waterways. In 1883, an even more daunting document appeared, this time a *Report from the Select Committee on Canals* (D) running to nearly 400 pages, but stiff with detail, including the verbatim evidence given to the Committee to assist its deliberations. Browsing through these, we find complaints which are still pertinent a century later:

> ...There is at the present time a large traffic with the Continent carried on entirely with sailing barges which can enter the Continental rivers and Continental canals, but are barred at of [sic] our own ports and cannot go inland at all.
> Q. And they come up the Thames?
> A. Yes, they come up the Thames as far as London; but they are unable to go on any of our canals...

Much of the same sort is to be found in the Report of the Royal Commission (already mentioned in Chapter 2). It has often been asserted that we have a system of government wise enough to appoint independent commissions to study difficult problems, but too foolish to be guided by their recommendations. This seems to be true of this Royal Commission at least, for its advice went virtually unheeded.

Apart from a number of reports on water conservancy and land drainage, the next major official publication was a report to the British Transport Commission in 1955 – *Canals and Inland Waterways: report of the Board of Survey* (C) often referred to as the 'Rusholme Report' after the Board's Chairman, Lord Rusholme. This report, formally made in 1954 but not printed until the following year (twice), not surprisingly recommended bolder steps than Government were prepared to take. Nevertheless, a programme of track improvement was embarked upon, but seemed to fizzle out before reaching its £5.5 million goal. One idea was, however, endorsed: the division of the waterways into different classes according to their commercial potential. The British Transport Commission, established by the Transport Act 1947, was battling with the statutory obligation to divert profits from the successful waterways to the maintenance of many miles of virtually useless canal. Rusholme recommended that 1330 miles should be retained for transport use, and 771 miles should be written off as redundant and disposed of in the most convenient fashion. This last suggestion aroused the fury of, amongst others, the Inland Waterways Association, and in due course an (independent) Government Committee of Enquiry was appointed in 1956, under the Chairmanship of Leslie Bowes. The 'Bowes Report', *The Report of the Committee of Enquiry into Inland Waterways* (C), was published in 1958, and reprinted in 1960. It largely restates the views of the Rusholme Report, recommending a commitment to maintain a commercial system of 1315 miles for twenty-five years, and the enlargement of the Grand Union main line to 90-ton standard.

The way the waterways were administered changed from time to time after the Transport Act of 1947; our present British Waterways Board emerged from the dismembered British Transport Commission in 1962, and has proved a productive publisher since then. Perhaps its most significant works have been *The Future of the Waterways* (1964 – Grade B) and *The Facts about the Waterways* (1965 – Grade B). Amongst other things, these paved the way for the legal recognition of three classes of waterways in the 1968 Transport Act, and the disposal of BWB's narrow-boat fleets. This was a realistic step, but one of historic moment, as it marked the end of a nationwide freight carrying service on England's waterways.

42

Both BTC and BWB have issued annual reports and a lot of publicity material of all types. Much of the latter is truly ephemeral – embarrassingly common when issued, therefore not highly valued by the recipients, and therefore comparatively rare a few years later. Some, of course, is hardly worth preserving, but a number of the booklets are valuable records of the waterway scene and of the aspirations of those in charge. *British Waterways* (A) was published by the Docks & Inland Waterways Executive (part of BTC) in about 1951; its 32 pages contain 19 photos, many of which depict craft at work, and a useful summary of the services offered by BTC at that time. In 1957, British Transport Waterways (successors to DIWE) published a booklet *Display of Craft and Equipment* (A) in conjunction with an exhibition at Little Venice. There were 22 major exhibits, many of which were engineering craft and appliances, which rarely receive much attention. Amongst others, visitors could see a Bantam push-tug, a steam dredger, a floating hedge-cutter, a weed-cutter and an ice-breaker. Thus even slight publications can provide information or insights not readily available elsewhere.

Acts of Parliament

Waterway construction generally requires the acquisition of land, which the owners may not wish to sell, and the modification of local water flow patterns, which may appear to some local residents (e.g. millers, fishermen, farmers) as an interference with their natural rights. For these reasons, virtually every canal and navigation required one or more Acts of Parliament. A number of the river navigations were first authorised by Royal Charter, such as that granted to the City of York in 1462, which gave to the City powers to preserve the navigation of the Ouse and Humber, and several tributaries. However, Acts as such become the normal means of developing navigations after about the middle of the seventeenth century. Up to this point, about fifty Acts had been passed for rivers, but soon canals proper dominate the scene. Between 1750 and 1790, there were about 70 canal Acts for England alone, and this figure rose to over 200 for the period 1791-1810. Thereafter the rate declined; the total was only about 100 for the next twenty-year period. Parliamentary activity can not, of course, be judged in terms of Acts alone, as there were at all times Bills introduced which were not passed.

Anno sexto & septimo

Gulielmi III. Regis.

An Act to prevent Exactions of the Occupiers of Locks and Wears upon the River of *Thames* Westward, and for Ascertaining the Rates of Water-Carriage upon the said River.

hereas the Rivers of Thames and Isis have, Time out of Mind, been Navigable from the City of London to the Village of Bercott in the County of Oxford, and for divers

A Thames Act of the late seventeenth century.

44

There must in all be some 500 navigation Acts for the British Isles, and a full collection of these would be almost impossible to acquire. However as they have considerable interest, it is well worth trying to acquire a few, perhaps those relating to a particular locality or period. They are met with in several forms, but are most desirable as the first printing by the Crown Printers. As originally published, most Acts were on untrimmed sheets folded to foolscap size and, if of more than one sheet, crudely sewn together by being 'stabbed' with a coarse needle. The sewing is not through the fold of the paper (as in a sewn book) but through the front and back faces. Most Acts which have survived were bound up for lawyers or solicitors into complete volumes, each covering all or part of a Parliamentary Session. For a variety of reasons, these volumes are now trickling onto the market and are being broken up into their constituent Acts by dealers, usually specialists. Acts broken out of such volumes usually have traces of the binding, often even pieces of calf, adhering to the edge, but are usually in reasonable condition as they have spent a cosy life in a legal office, sandwiched between their fellows. Acts were occasionally reprinted by the Crown Printers, either singly or in groups, in foolscap. For convenience, some Acts, or groups relating to a particular subject, were reprinted in octavo, which makes for a much more manageable volume. The first two Barnsley Canal Acts (1793 and 1808) were reprinted in this way in 1826, and the first three Bridgewater Canal Acts under which construction actually took place (1759. 1760 and 1762) were printed in octavo by 'Mark Baskett, Printer to the King's most Excellent Majesty; and by the Assigns of Robert Baskett' in 1762. During Victorian times, the paper size was reduced to quarto, and during the 20th century we have come down to a much more realistic octavo size for the original printings.

The identification of earlier Acts is not altogether straightforward, as they were originally numbered in a sequence which related to the monarch's regnal year and the Parliamentary Session. A typical eighteenth-century Act might be designated 15 Geo III cap 8 – shorthand for 'the eighth Chapter (or Act) of the 15th year of the reign of George III'. There are also various types of Act, e.g. Public, Local & Personal, and Private, which have different numbering rules, and these rules have been changed from time to time. Add to this the fact that earlier Acts have neither their chapter numbers nor dates printed on them, and the complications arising when the Parliamentary sessions did not coincide with the regnal years, to say nothing of the fact that mistakes were sometimes made by the Parliamentary clerks, and you have a recipe for confusion. It is hardly surprising that legal matters are complicated, if there is no agreement about which law is which! Having pointed out some of the dangers, I can do no better than suggest assistance in the form of a solid reference book like the *Chronological Table of the Statutes* which may be found lurking in the reference section of your local public library. P.Stevenson, writing in the January 1965 issue of the *Journal of the Railway and Canal Historical Society* provides a good introduction to the peculiarities of Act citation between 1811 and 1946, but do also look at the errors in his article, listed in the July 1965 issue. For waterways alone, Priestley's *Historical Account of the Navigable Rivers, Canals, and Railways* (see Chapter 2) is the easiest reference source, but beware! Not only does Priestley make a few errors of commission and omission but he fails to distinguish between the different types of Act, and, of course, does not extend his coverage to Ireland.

If there are hardships, what of the joys of collecting Acts? Firstly, they offer the cheapest way of acquiring genuine contemporary material – at Grade A, B or C they are far cheaper, these days, than the books, share certificates or other printed survivors of the Canal Age. Secondly, particularly the earlier Acts are interesting pieces of printing, set in Black Letter (until 1793), with engraved coats of Arms, and ornamental initial letters. Thirdly, they are historical documents, and much of the history of a navigation may be learnt from a study of its Acts. Taking the Thames as an outstanding example, we find that it had 33 Acts between 1695 and 1829, and as Acts are rarely less than 4, and often over 20, pages long, we see that the Acts provide a good start for a study of Thames navigation history. Three reasons should be good enough for anyone, but if a fourth were needed, Acts can provide a contemporary view of the way in which the industry developed. Particularly useful are those Acts which do not relate to individual navigations, but to more general matters, e.g. 35 Geo III c58, *An Act for requiring all Boats, Barges, and other Vessels...on Navigable Rivers, and on Inland Navigations, in Great Britain, to be registered*; 8 & 9 Vict c42, *An Act to enable Canal Companies to become Carriers of Goods upon their Canals*; and 40 & 41 Vict c60, *The Canal Boats Act, 1877*. This last represented a considerable victory for George Smith, whose campaigning on behalf of the canal boatmen is described in Chapter 3.

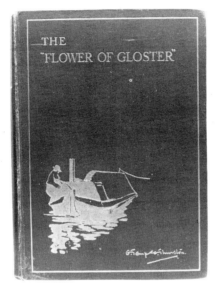

Two early narrow-boat cruises: Thurston's *The "Flower of Gloster"* (1911) and Cotes' *Two Girls on a Barge* (1891).

A selection of modern waterway guides.

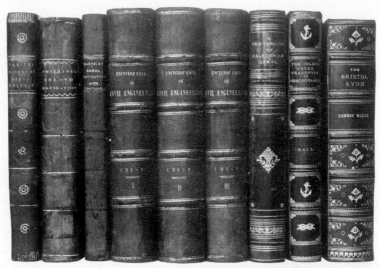

Contemporary leather: Skrine's *Rivers of Great Britain* (1801), Phillips' *General History* (4th edn, 1803), reprint of two Barnsley Canal Acts (1826), Cresy's *Encyclopaedia of Civil Engineering* (1847), *A Trip Through the Caledonian Canal* by 'Bumps' (1861), Hall's *The Inland Water Transport in Mesopotamia* (1921), and Walls' *The Bristol Avon* (1927).

'The Inland Waterways Histories' series in dustwrapper. Note the non-uniform designs of *The Yorkshire Ouse* (the first of the series) and *The Trent & Mersey* (which is, in error, in the style of 'The Canals of the British Isles' series).

Two classics of war-time boating.

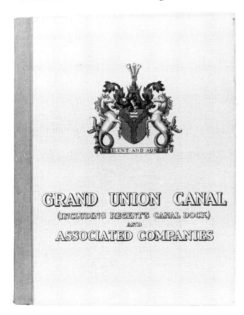

Two commercial handbooks from the 1930s.

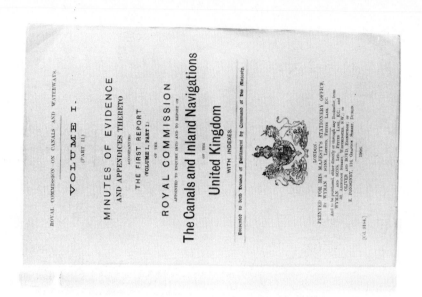

One of the many volumes of the Royal Commission's report.

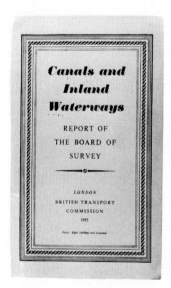

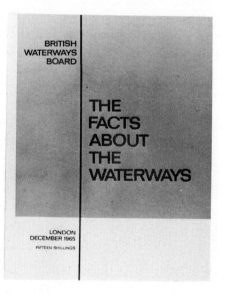

Two important post-war reports.

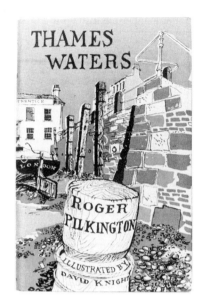

The first of the 'Small Boat' series: 1956 and 1957.

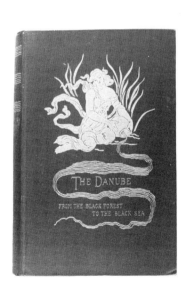

Same river, different styles: 1892 and 1938 (that on the left is by F.D.Millett).

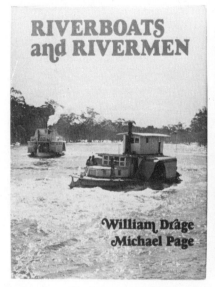

Two striking dustwrappers, showing the Murray River and the Nile.

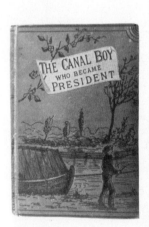
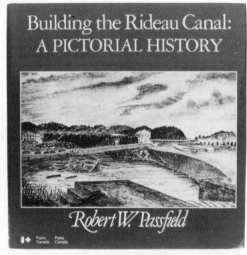

Ancient and Modern for North America. On the left is Frederic Gammon's biography of Garfield (c1881).

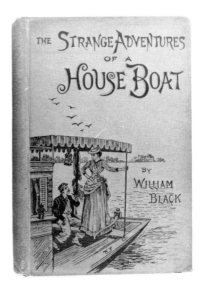

Adult fiction: a fine dustwrapper from 1930, and a three-decker in cloth from 1888.

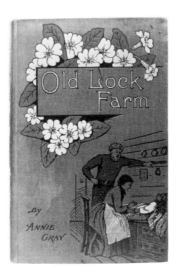

Children's fiction of 1888 and 1970.

A postcard showing Anderton Lift before reconstruction, flanked by salt chutes.

Medallions commemorating the opening of the Manchester Ship Canal in 1894.

Chapter 5

WATERWAYS IN EUROPE

The literature (in English) relating to waterways in Europe has not developed in the same way as that for our own waterways. Englishmen have seen Europe's rivers and canals almost exclusively from the cruising point of view, with the result that cruising guides and accounts abound, unleavened by a single systematic history of the waterways of any country, or of Europe as a whole. There are, of course, many topographical works on European rivers, especially the Rhine and the Danube, but navigation is often only a minor component of these. Amongst the few historical works which do exist are Tom Rolt's *From Sea to Sea: the Canal du Midi* (1973 – Grade BC), surprisingly scarce in view of the author's reputation at the time of publication, Timothy Holme's *Gondola, Gondolier* (1971 – Grade A), and Riccardo Pergoli's *The Boats of Venice* (1981), a lavish work on all the special craft of Venice, still in print at Grade C. Eric de Maré's *Swedish Cross Cut* (1964 – Grade C) does contain some history, but is primarily intended as a topographical work. The history of a modern project is found in *The White Sea Canal* (D), a work of multiple authorship which was published in an English translation in 1935. However, before relying too heavily on its contents, first read Alexander Solzhenitzyn's *The Gulag Archipelago Part 2*. His account of the construction is written from, to say the least, a different viewpoint. He also records that following political changes in Moscow, most of the original Russian copies of *The White Sea Canal* were destroyed, so its survival in English translation is of some significance.

For the best systematically compiled and presented information on European waterways, you must turn (as long as you don't want anything particularly recent) to an unlikely source – the Naval Intelligence Divison of the Admiralty. In 1915, a Geographical Section was formed within the Division, and during the second World War, this Section was called upon to produce *Geographical Handbooks* for each of a large number of countries, describing their geology, climate, history, resources, communications (including waterways), and so on. Numerous professional and academic geographers were drafted in to assist, and very compendious were the results. *The Handbook for Belgium*, for example, runs to 693 pages, with many maps, photos etc, and one chapter is devoted to waterways. Several countries required two or three volumes. Although originally 'restricted', many of these handbooks have come onto the market in recent years at BC (per volume).

Cruising

Cruising naturally pre-dates cruising guides, but the earliest accounts of Continental journeys are (just as in Britain) those describing trips on commercially operated passenger boats. An early example is Robert Southey's *Journal of a tour in the Netherlands in the Autumn of 1815* (D) in which Southey briefly recounts two *trekschuit* trips in Belgium in September .1815. This journal wasn't published until 1902, years after his death in 1843 and the sale of his papers in 1864.

Mechanical power, in the form of the steam engine, was initially only available on a largish scale, and thus its first applications were to passenger vessels rather than to private craft. During the early nineteenth century, an extensive system of paddle-steamer routes was developed, and one early passenger was Michael Quin, whose descent of the Danube in 1834 from Budapest to Ruse (and many further travels in the region as well) is described in *A Steam Voyage Down the Danube...* (2 vols, 1835). The book was obviously well received, going to 3 editions, and an American edition, within two years. Any of these would be Grade EF. Encouraged by its success, he went on to write *Steam Voyages on the Seine, the Moselle, and the Rhine...* (2 vols, 1843 – Grade EF) in which he included narratives of a trip from London to Paris on a succession of steamers, a short trip down the Moselle from Trier to Koblenz, and a third up the Rhine from Koblenz to Mainz. No further editions were published, possibly partly due to Quin's untimely death while working on the proofs in 1843.

I haven't yet found any English book which describes a private cruise on the Continent earlier than 1832. In that year, Elizabeth Strutt went down the Loire from Tours to Nantes in a small boat, 'large enough to accommodate eight persons'. Fifty francs were paid for the boat, 'including oars, chairs, table, and awning'. The trip is recorded in *Six weeks on the Loire* published anonymously in 1833 (D). Few navigation details are given, although it is interesting to note that the boat was purchased because 'the steam-boat was not likely to present itself at the time we wished'.

The first cruise genuinely undertaken for its own sake and written up as a book comes somewhat later, in 1852. This was *The log of the Water Lily (four-oared Thames gig) during a rowing excursion on the Rhine, and other streams of Germany* by Robert Mansfield. Not a neat title, but at least it tells you what the book's about, which is more than some I could name. Why Mansfield published this anonymously I don't know, but he merely demurely described himself as 'an Oxford Man and a Wykehamist' (i.e. jolly good chap all round). The following year he published, again anonymously, *The Water Lily on the Danube: being a brief account of the perils of a pair-oar during a voyage from Lambeth to Pesth*. The two accounts were then put together, and the combined volume published under Mansfield's name as a 'second edition' in 1854. The publisher was Cooke, but when a third edition appeared in the same year, apparently printed from some of the same type, the publisher had changed to Ingram. A Tauchnitz edition is also dated 1854. Before the fifth edition was issued in 1873 Mansfield added the log of a third trip, this one in France, and changed the title to *The Log of the Water Lily during three cruises on the Rhine, Neckar, Main, Moselle, Danube, Saône and Rhone*. There was at least one more edition, in 1877, but despite these numerous printings, any copy should be Grade D.

Again anonymously, Edmund George Harvey wrote *Our Cruise in the Undine, the journal of an English pair-oar expedition through France, Baden, Rhenish Bavaria, Prussia and Belgium* (1854 – Grade D). There was then a bit of a gap until 1866, when the great John MacGregor's *A thousand miles in the Rob Roy canoe on rivers and lakes of Europe* was first published (see also Chapter 1). The canoe used, designed by MacGregor, was effectively an all-wood version of the kayak, complete with a small sail, and its length of 15 feet was chosen to allow it entry to German railway wagons. The book was an instant success – as was the idea of canoeing – and ran to at least 21 editions. There were two American editions, and a facsimile of the 13th was published by the British Canoe Union in 1963. Not surprisingly, it comes in various shapes and sizes, and the price varies accordingly. I have never seen a first edition, and would put this at Grade CD, but a good copy of one of the later editions, some of which have a delightful picture of the canoeist in the middle of a herd of swimming cattle on the Meuse, would be Grade B, and the less desirable editions, some of which lack the Appendix, would be down to Grade A.

MacGregor set the fashion, and until the first World War, every summer saw Englishmen exploring virtually every bit of navigable water in Europe, although it was generally agreed that the ideal cruise was down a river, and that canals were to be avoided if possible. Picking out a few highlights, we find Robert Louis Stevenson's *Inland Voyage*, whose success set Stevenson's feet firmly on the literary ladder, first appearing in 1878. Numerous editions exist, some illustrated, and their price would be Grade A to C, depending on quality. In 1885, a charming quarto volume *The Wanderings of the Beetle* by E.P.Warren and C.F.M.Cleverly, described an inrigged pair-oar trip in France and Belgium. I have a particularly soft spot for *The Beetle*, as this was the first waterway book I ever bought. It cost me two shillings of my pocket money, in the old covered market in Inverness, and time has shown it to have been a very lucky find, as it is rarely seen, and is Grade D.

The *Beetle* shoots a mill.

Another rarity is a book by an Oxford don, Lewis Farnell, describing his various small-boat trips in *An Englishman's Adventures on German Rivers* (1891). It is unusual, presumably unique, in that Farnell sold the copyright in his diaries of the trips to Oberlehrer Dr.A.Hamann, for £5, so that these might be used to prepare a reading text for German schoolchildren. The two results were that Farnell became well known and much hated by numerous Germans who had been forced through *An Englishman's Adventures* at an impressionable age, and that the book is very scarce in England. Doubtless in Germany it is a staple of the jumble sale bookstall, just as our own stalls groan under Hall & Knight's *Elementary Algebra* and inky copies of bowdlerised Shakespeare texts, but it is Grade C material in Farnell's homeland.

An American, Poultney Bigelow, made up a party of three canoeists to descend the Danube, and two books resulted, both in 1892: his own *Paddles and Politics Down the Danube* (Grade C) and F.D.Millet's more impressive *The Danube from the Black Forest to the Black Sea* (D), some issues of which have a beautiful silver and gilt cover. Both were published virtually simultaneously in New York and London. The only woman to write about a trip of this sort, and presumably one of the first to undertake one, was Mrs Josef Alexander Donner, whose *Down the Danube in an Open Boat* (c.1894) would be Grade D. The 'open boat' she and her husband used in their descent from Ratisbon (now Regensburg) to Pressburg (now Bratislava) was the *Praealtus*, a 12ft 6in sailing boat built in Venice from lemon wood and pine. Arthur Koebel should get the long distance prize for his *Dinghey Dawdle: Danubian and other. From Thames to Black Sea* (1902 – Grade CD), but also the

CHAPTER I.

Life in the „Alles mit" on the Neckar, Rhine, and Moselle.

On Friday August the 4th 1885 the five Englishmen who wished to return to the nomad life of their forefathers, and to study the Neckar, the Rhine, and the Moselle from the thwarts [1]) of an Oxford four [2]), met at Victoria Station [3]), and the adventure was fairly begun. The night on the sea was magnificent,

---

[1]) Die Ruderbänke. — [2]) a four, ein vierrubriges Boot. — [3]) Victoria Station, die Hauptstation im Westen von London, um nach dem Kontinent zu reisen. — [4]) und verteilten die Ämter. — [5]) ganz augenscheinlich. —

Farnell's diary transmogrified.

literary boot for making such an exciting journey into such dull reading. The advent of steam, paraffin and petrol engines did not manage to eliminate the canoeist, although I think we've seen the last of the four-oars and inrigged pairs. Melville Chater did some extensive conoeing in the 1920s, and in 1932 produced *Two Canoe Gypsies: their eight-hundred-mile canal voyage through Belgium, Brittany, Touraine, Gascony and Languedoc: being an account of backdoor life on bargeman's highway* (Grade D). The canoe was called *Nageoma*, which I'd always assumed was an authentic North American Indian name, until I realised he was backed by the *National Geographic Magazine*. In 1935 came Rowland Raven-Hart's *Canoe Errant* (B) describing very extensive cruising on Europe's rivers, the first of his full-length canoeing books. In recent years, Gabriel Seal's *Canoe Touring Abroad* (1969 – Grade A) and John Wilson's *Canoeing Down the Rhone* (1957 – Grade A) show that the spirit of MacGregor lives on.

Rowed craft were ideal for exploring the least navigable of the rivers, but their occupants rarely carried all their kit with them, instead having this sent from one riverside hotel to the next by railway. Although it limited the routes available, the use of a larger craft gave the voyager both more independence while cruising, and the ability to take himself across the Channel. It was the former which moved Philip Hamerton, a distinguished artist, to hire a *berrichon* for a lengthy journey down the Saône. He had already taken the frailest of craft – a paper canoe – down the Arroux, a tiny tributary stream of the Loire, and recorded the feat in *The Unknown River* (1871 – Grade D). His Saône trip was to be a much more organised affair, and he needed a more spacious vessel for the job. The *berrichon*, named after the Canal du Berry, was (by Continental standards) a small barge, about 90 feet long, and 9 feet in the beam. It was towed by one donkey, which lived on board. Hamerton was accompanied by another artist, Joseph Pennell, and the book *The Saône: a summer voyage* (1887) contains 148 illustrations by these two. They used the *berrichon*, named the *Boussemroum*, for the first part of their journey, then transhipped to Hamerton's own catamaran, the *Arar*, at Chalon, to complete the descent to Lyons. *The Saône* was published in an ordinary edition (Grade DE) and a large paper edition, limited to 275 copies, which is Grade E. There were also American editions in 1888 and 1897 (both D).

A most remarkable voyage was accomplished by Henry Doughty in the Norfolk wherry *Gipsy*. This was towed to Stavoren in 1888, and spent the next 14 years in foreign parts. Some of her travels are recorded for us in Doughty's *Friesland Meres and through the Netherlands: the voyage of a family in a Norfolk wherry* (1889 – Grade C) and *Our Wherry in Wendish lands: from Friesland, through the Mecklenburg lakes, to Bohemia* (c.1892 – Grade D). There were four editions of the former, and two of the latter. For those who aren't sure where Bohemia is, let me merely reveal that they actually just got into what is now Czechoslovakia – an extraordinary feat for a wherry. The next wherry to attempt the crossing of the North Sea, the *Elsie*, foundered under tow, yet *Gipsy* duly returned to home waters and saw continued service on the Broads. *Our Wherry* is a difficult book to acquire, as its Continental coverage has ensured it a ready market in Germany in recent years. Nevertheless, it is a book worth pursuing, not only for its contents, but also for its fine cover, which uses inlaid cloth of different colours to build up a richly coloured flag.

They could all draw and sketch, these Victorians, and usually illustrated their books themselves. The same is also true of Donald Maxwell, now well-known for his 'Unknown County' series. In his younger days, he wrote and illustrated two fine books recording his Continental boating experiences. Both are deservedly Grade D, and would lend distinction to any bookcase. The first, *The Log of the Griffin: the story of a cruise from the Alps to the Thames* (1905), has a delightful cover depicting, in the most delicate of colour printing, two horses pulling a boat on a cart up an Alp, over the sub-title *From Switzerland to Teddington*. The extraordinary fact is that Maxwell had the *Griffin* built to his own design in Brunnadern, a Swiss village some twenty miles from any navigable water, and after surviving numerous perils arrived at last at Teddington in November 1901. Despite the loss of the *Griffin* in a storm in 1903, Maxwell had developed a taste for Continental waters, and in 1905 took a small sailing boat, the *Walrus*, up the Rhine, through the Ludwigs Canal, and down the Danube to the Black Sea. Again there were adventures, including twice being arrested as a spy, and these are all in *A Cruise Across Europe* (1907), one of my favourite books, endearing for its route, its illustrations and the modesty of its author in his decriptions of this exceptional journey of great length and difficulty, which ended with his contracting malaria before arrival at the Black Sea. Only one other Englishman has sailed across Europe by water – Merlin Minshall, who went the 'long way', up the Seine rather than the Rhine, and then via the Ludwigs Canal to the Danube. This trip was described in the *National Geographic Magazine* in 1937, and later in his autobiography *Guilt-edged* (1975).

Luxury, or some would even say comfort, on Continental cruises awaited the arrival of mechanical power. First came the steam engine, and with it a few scarce books like W.J.C.Moens' *Through France and Belgium, by river and canal, in the steam yacht 'Ytene'* (1876 – Grade D), and G.Christopher Davies' *On Dutch Waterways. The cruise of the S.S. Atalanta on the rivers & canals of Holland and the north of Belgium* (1887). The latter occurs in two distinct issues: the first has a leaf ix/x listing the illustrations, the more common, and presumably later, issue has no leaf ix/x and has eleven gaps in the pagination, where (single-sided) plates should be located but aren't. The publishers of this large quarto volume found, I suppose, that sales were not covering costs, and were forced to economise by omitting the plates. With plates this would be Grade D, without Grade CD.

Besides Minshall's, the only other book describing a trans-Europe trip 'the long way' is Henry Rowland's *Across Europe in a motor boat* (1908). Both this edition and the 1915 reprint are Grade D. Rowland had the *Beaver* built in London, and then set off on perhaps the most ambitious waterway trip ever planned – up the Seine, through three canals to the Rhine, to the Danube via the Ludwigs Canal, and then south through the Black Sea to the Bosphorus, through the Mediterranean to Marseilles, via the Canal du Midi and the Garonne to France's Atlantic coast, and then north to the Seine, ending up in Paris, some 7,000 miles later. As it was, their exciting journey ended with total wreck in the Black Sea, and the crew were lucky to escape with their lives.

Showing how to do it in style, the chemist Sir Edward Thorpe took his 100 foot motor yacht *Cysne* up the Seine, as he describes in *The Seine from Havre to Paris* (1913). Although quite a handsome production, the book has too much of the Baedeker about it, and is only Grade B. This is perhaps surprising when we consider that Thorpe also wrote *A Yachtsman's Guide to the Dutch Waterways* published in 1905 (B) with new editions in 1931 and 1954 (both A). Another man who managed to be pretty comfortable while cruising was the novelist Arnold Bennett. He should have written about the Trent & Mersey, or the Caldon, but as he lived in France for much of his life, it was European canals to which he turned his attention. *From the Log of the Velsa* (1914 – Grade D) describes a number of his trips, including some on the canals of Holland, and the rivers of East Anglia. The *Velsa* was built on the lines of a Dutch fishing-smack, 55 feet long and 15 feet in the beam.

'Her supreme advantage, from my point of view, is that she has well over six feet of head-room in the saloon and in the sleeping-cabins... Further, she carries a piano and an encyclopedia, two necessaries of life. I may say that I have never known another yacht that carried an encyclopedia in more than a score of volumes.'

The first edition was published in New York and is bound in blue cloth bearing a coloured picture of the Velsa on the front. It is quite scarce, but the American facsimile of 1975 (B) is easier to find, but is bound, alas, in a horrid brown oilcloth. I presume the choice is dictated by the fact that it is a library edition, as the Americans have shown the greatest reluctance to descend to the pitted paper binding which is used for most British hardbacks, and have instead remained faithful to real cloth.

Another novelist, Cecil Scott Forester, has left us accounts of his cruises. In *The Voyage of the Annie Marble* (1929), he describes a cruise up the Seine, through the canals, and down the Loire, in a punt-built dinghy, 15 feet by 5 feet, with a canvas camping cover and a 4 HP outboard. This was called the *Annie Marble* after the leading lady of *Payment Deferred*, one of his first novels (and well worth reading). He stresses the great economy achieved by this mode of travel, providing accounts totalling under £60 for eleven weeks' cruising for him and his wife, including their fares to and from France, the carriage of the boat, and hotels while awaiting its arrival. Sacré Bleu! They enjoyed the experience so much that next year they went to Germany. As *Annie Marble's* home port was Kew, Forester had the good idea of loading all their gear into the boat, and taking her straight down to the docks, where she was lifted onto the deck of a small freighter bound for Hamburg. Here she was lowered into the water, and off the Foresters went for a 16-week cruise (total cost under £85) which took them as far east as Stettin, which is now the Polish town of Szczecin. Surprisingly for a man who read a book a day, Forester had never come across Doughty's *Wherry in Wendish Lands*, for he writes:

'I firmly believe, as a matter of fact, that ours was the first [Red Ensign] to be seen in all Mecklenburg... If any Englishman who reads this book has navigated the Mecklenburg lakes, or knows any other Englishman who has done so, I beg him most earnestly to write to me and tell me so'.

I wonder if anyone did? Despite Forester's later successes, neither book has ever been reprinted, and collectors of Modern Firsts (a powerful market force) have pushed the price of both well into Grade D.

Since the second World War, many yachtsmen have regarded continental waterways (particularly those of France) largely as a way to get to the Mediterranean. This has resulted in a rash of yachting books in which inland cruising plays a small, and often rather scorned, part. In strong contrast, the same period has thrown up Dr Roger Pilkington, a man who has made a career of exploring Europe's waterways and publishing the results. His 'Small Boat' series is quite remarkable in that he wrote 18 books between 1956 and 1971, and they have a uniformity of production rarely met with outside 'collected editions'. Two describe boating on the Thames, and the remainder cover an enormous area of Western Europe. The first is simply *Thames Waters* and all the others are called *Small Boat to, up, on* or *through* somewhere. The full list in order of publication is: *Thames Waters, Belgium, Holland, Skagerrak, Alsace, Sweden, Bavaria, Germany, Southern France, France, Thames, Meuse, Luxembourg, Moselle, Northern Germany, Elsinore, Lower Rhine*, and *Upper Rhine*. Several went into two or three impressions, at least one into paperback, and two were reprinted as rather mean facsimiles by Ian Henry. Most are Grade A, but some are much rarer than others, and would reach Grade B.

Of the couple of dozen other cruising books, only three will be mentioned here. These are Robert Gibbings' *Coming Down the Seine* (1953 – Grade B), because he finished his journey on the *Yarvic*, a boat which ferried Pan books from the Paris printers to London, John Marriner's *Afloat in Europe* (1967 – Grade A) because he got into Eastern Germany and Poland, and Ethelbert M.Robinson's *The Sailor's Foot* (1954 – Grade AB). This last is noteworthy because it is the only waterway book I've ever read in which the author complains continually about everything, and seems to have extracted no pleasure from a journey through France by river and canal. Add a title which tells you nothing, and you have avoided a best-seller.

Continental Reference

There are few works of reference on continental waterways which are at all readable. Most are merely designed to pack in a lot of information for the prospective yachtsman, probably going through to the Mediterranean anyway. Thorpe's *Yachtsman's Guide to the Dutch Waterways* (1905) has already been mentioned. *Cruising in the Netherlands. A Handbook to certain of the rivers and canals of Holland, Friesland, and the North of Belgium* (1894 – Grade C) by G.Christopher Davies is more of a log than a handbook, being based on three trips by the author, the first of which was written up as *On Dutch Waterways*, mentioned previously. Later guides include a series by E.E.Benest, published by Imray, Laurie, Norie & Wilson. The series comprises *Inland Waterways of France* (1956), *of Belgium* (1960), and *of the Netherlands* (in three volumes 1966 – 1971), all of which have been revised from time to time. Any copy of the various editions would be Grade AB, as would copies of the other series, written by Philip Bristow. These are *Through the French Canals* (1970), *Through the Belgian Canals* (1972), *Through the Dutch Canals* (1974) and *Through the German Waterways* (1975). Roger Pilkington's *Waterways in Europe* (1974 – Grade A) is a useful starter, being the distillation of a very great deal of personal experience. All these guides are more useful than readable. If you are looking for something more entertaining, try John Liley's *France – The Quiet Way* (1975 – Grade B) and *Barge Country: an exploration of the Netherlands Waterways* (1980 – Grade B), both of which make excellent reading while still conveying a lot of useful information. Extending far beyond cruising is Roger Calvert's very thorough *Inland Waterways of Europe* (1963 – Grade B). The author sets out to record a good deal about the commercial uses of the waterways he describes, which marks his book out from many others. It was reprinted in 1975 (Grade AB), but the opportunity to produce a revised edition was not taken, and twelve years' developments were squeezed into a couple of new pages at the front. Hugh McKnight's *The Guinness Guide to Waterways of Western Europe* (1978 – Grade C) is an enjoyable *mélange* of history, topography and cruising advice, decorated with a large number of Hugh's excellent photographs. Its geographical coverage is, however, poor; one third of the book is given to the British Isles, and only five countries are described in the remainder (France, Germany, Belgium, Holland and Sweden). It does contain a good bibliography. On the commercial side, the way in which the waterways of France, Belgium, Germany and the Netherlands are run as successful transport systems is well described in *Report on Continental Waterways* (A) published in 1975 after a great deal of on-the-spot research by David Edwards-May, necessarily an able linguist. Information about Eastern Europe is difficult to acquire, but one good source exists for the USSR. This is *Soviet Waterways* (C) by Andrei Lebed and Boris Yakovlev, published in 1956 by The Institute for the Study of the USSR, in Munich. Some engineering and vessel details can be gleaned from papers published by PIANC, especially those for their 1977 quadrennial congress, which was held in Leningrad.

Chapter 6

OTHER FOREIGN WATERWAYS

North America

Not many books about North American waterways are available in this country, though they are thicker on the ground in the bookshops of Canada and the USA. Nevertheless, the literature on the waterways of North America is not nearly so extensive or thorough as that for Britain, although there are some good histories of individual waterways.

For Canada, Robert Legget's *Canals of Canada* (1976 – Grade B) provides the best comprehensive introduction. It is the sole representative of a 'Canals of the World' series which David & Charles hoped to publish, but didn't. The only other book I know with a broad coverage of Canada is William Kingsford's *The Canadian Canals*, published in Toronto in 1865, and therefore not surprisingly Grade D. Legget also detailed the history of the Rideau Canal, built by a British Army officer as a defensive measure against the United States, in *Rideau Waterway*. This was first published in 1955, but reprinted at least four times, and was also available as a paperback. Copies are not hard to find, and are Grade AB. May 1982 was the Rideau's 150th birthday, an occasion marked by the publication of several commemorative books. Robert Passfield's *Building the Rideau Canal*, published by Parks Canada, the canal's present curators, is particularly well illustrated, containing 73 contemporary watercolours, drawings and maps, of which 46 are reproduced in colour.

Canada's major waterway system – the Saint Lawrence Seaway and the Great Lakes to which it gives access – was developed over a long period, and has predictably been the subject of a number of substantial works, mostly published in Canada, e.g. Guy Lindsay's *The Great Lakes – St Lawrence Deep Waterway* (1949 – Grade BC), Major Cowan's *The Welland Ship Canal between Lake Ontario and Lake Erie, 1913 – 1932* (1935 – Grade CD), George Stephens' *The St Lawrence Waterway Project* (1929 – Grade D) and William Willoughby's *The St Lawrence Waterway: a study in politics and diplomacy* (1961 – Grade B).

One of the classics of United States canal history is *A Description of*

A

DESCRIPTION

OF THE

CANALS AND RAIL ROADS

OF THE

UNITED STATES,

COMPREHENDING

NOTICES OF ALL THE WORKS

OF

INTERNAL IMPROVEMENT

THROUGHOUT

THE SEVERAL STATES.

BY H. S. TANNER.

NEW YORK:
T. R. TANNER & J. DISTURNELL,
124 BROADWAY.

———

1840.

Virtually an American 'Priestley', this has also been reprinted in facsimile.

67

the Canals and Rail roads of the United States, comprehending notices of all the works of internal improvement throughout the several states by Henry Tanner. Originally published in 1840, this is virtually an American Priestley, and I expect it would be about the same price, although I have never seen a first edition offered for sale. Fortunately for scholars, it was reprinted in facsimile by Augustus M.Kelley in 1970 (Grade C). Herbert Quick's *American Inland Waterways* (1909) is an exceptionally well illustrated book, with 73 pages of photographs, and a fine cover, and is deservedly Grade E. Alvin F.Harlow's *Old Towpaths: the story of the American Canal Era* (1926 – Grade E) was rightly deemed worth reprinting in 1964, but copies of both editions are scarce in Britain. It is a useful historical work, containing 13 pages of bibliography, and 47 pages of photographs, with such delights as mules, the inclined planes of the Morris Canal, and an experiment in barge traction using electric locos on the towpath. One frustration is the lack of an index, a piece of unforgivable cheese-paring which not even the reprinters thought to rectify.

There are also books about particular waterways, and the Mississippi must have the largest score of these, with the Erie Canal, together with its 20th century counterpart, the New York State Barge Canal, leading the canal field. Many of the books inspired by the Mississippi have dwelt lovingly upon the stern-wheelers, which so potently evoke the atmosphere of the mid-west in the nineteenth century. Harry Sinclair Drago's *The Steamboaters: from the early side-wheelers to the Big Packets* (1967 – Grade B) is a typical example, though not particularly well illustrated. The Erie Canal's early years are told in *Erie Water West: a history of the Erie Canal 1792 - 1854* by Ronald Shaw (1966 – Grade B), and the birth of its big brother is chronicled in great detail by Frank M.Williams in his *History of the Barge Canal of New York State* (1922 – Grade D). Don't think that because this was issued as a supplement to the *Annual Report of the State Engineer and Surveyor* it must be a thin and wispy item. Nothing could be further from the truth; it has 610 pages and 30 pages of photographs, and tells you all you want to know – possibly even more. Thomas Hahn's *Towpath Guide to the C & O Canal* (1974) is a detailed analysis of the remains of the Chesapeake & Ohio, published in four parts by the American Canal & Transportation Centre. Hahn has followed this with the *C & O Boatman 1892-1924* (1982) from the same publishers. Personal tastes are catered for by specialist books of various types. Mark Twain's much reprinted *Life on the Mississippi* gives the flavour of the old steamboating days. A first edition might be Grade DE, but reprints are easily found at Grade A. Serious students of inland shipping should seek out a copy of *The Origin and Development of the Waterways Policy of the United States* by William and Robert Hull (1967 – Grade BC), and the connoisseur of small-boat trips will also find scope for collection. A Victorian example, very much in the European tradition, is *Boating Trips on New England Rivers* (1884 – Grade C), and who could resist a title like *The Dingbat of Arcady*? Tempting though it is, you have to open the covers to find that it is Marguerite Wilkinson's account of journeying by small boat on the rivers of the west coast of the USA, published in 1922. It is only Grade A, because it is exactly the kind of book which, although non-fiction, is likely to be shelved in the fiction section (or even in the 20p tray), dragged down by its unilluminating title and lack of illustrations. Our own Raven-Hart descended the Mississippi, as *Canoe Errant on the Mississippi* (1938 – Grade B) records, and the most recent English travellers to publish a book about inland waterway travels in North America are Charles and Alice Mary Hadfield. In three months, they clocked up about 5,000 waterway miles, all using scheduled passenger services. Their chatty but informative *Afloat in America* (1979 – Grade A) contains some splendid asides – including the revelation that the Mississippi's last surviving 'original' steam-packet, *Delta Queen*, was in fact built on the Clyde!

Suez and Panama

Although they aren't the world's only ship canals, these two are by far the most important, and both have had continuing effects, not only on world trade, but also on world politics. Suez was built by Ferdinand de Lesseps, and opened on his 64th birthday, in November 1869. Being lockless, its construction was a triumph of diplomacy, organisation and earth-shifting. Several competent recent histories exist, e.g. *The Making of the Suez Canal* (1964) by John Marlowe, *Between two seas: the Creation of the Suez Canal* (1968), and John Pudney's *Suez: De Lesseps' Canal* (1968). All are Grade B and fairly common. The first two are primarily concerned with the events leading up to 1869, whereas Pudney continues his account right up to Egypt's nationalisation of the canal in 1956. Numerous more specialist works are available for those wanting something more than these broad accounts; for example, some of the builder's early trials and triumphs may be followed in *The Suez Canal. Letters and Documents descriptive of its rise and progress in*

1854 – 1856. The English translation, published in 1876, is Grade CD. A sound political and economic study is provided by Lt-Col. Sir Arnold Wilson in his *The Suez Canal: its past, present, and future* (1933 – Grade B), and a short but interesting period of Suez history is covered by Sir Norman Kipping in *The Suez Contractors* (1969 – Grade AB). Under a treaty of 1936, the Suez Canal was manned by British troops stationed in the 'canal zone'; in 1954, deteriorating relations with Egypt led to a new treaty, under which British private enterprise (in the shape of Suez Contractors Ltd) was to run the canal for seven years. Sir Norman describes their history up to its abrupt end in October 1956.

The history of the Panama Canal has been no less dramatic than that of Suez. Originally undertaken by de Lesseps as a sea-level canal in 1879, it was abandoned by his French company after ten years' struggle against difficulty and disease. In 1904, the first construction workers from the United States arrived in Panama, and ten years later the canal was officially opened. There is an enormous literature of the early years, including many reports on different routes across the isthmus. Panama has been much more of an American pre-occupation than a British one, and therefore the majority of the publications are American, although there is a sizeable British literature. For example, C.Reginald Enock's *The Panama Canal* (c.1914 – Grade A), written during construction, foresaw a rosy future for the canal, whereas John Foster Fraser ends his *Panama and What it Means* (1913 – Grade B) with a sceptical chapter entitled 'What is the use of it all?'. The best recent account of the building of the canal is David McCullough's *The Path Between the Seas: the creation of the Panama Canal, 1870 – 1914* (B), which was published in New York in 1977, but has arrived in Britain in largish numbers in recent years. As with Suez, most writers concentrate on the planning and construction of the canal, and it is not so easy to find histories covering the later years. A few have been written – for example Walter La Feber's *The Panama Canal: the crisis in historical perspective* (AB), published by Oxford University Press in New York in 1978.

The Rest of the World

In Asia most inland navigation is performed on lakes or unimproved rivers, and the literature is sparse. Lyn Harrington's *The Grand Canal of China* is a very scrappy book on a fascinating waterway, and deserves mention only because there is so little else. Originally published in

Chicago in 1967, it was republished in Britain in 1974, and is Grade A. J.O.P.Bland's *Houseboat Days in China* (1909 – Grade CD) gives something of the flavour of Chinese waterways, but is not intended as a systematic account of inland navigation in China. This does really seem to be a subject awaiting an author.

Elsewhere in Asia the ubiquitous Raven-Hart pops up again – this time in *Canoe to Mandalay* (1941 – Grade B) in which his travels down the Irawaddy are chronicled. There are of course many miles of canals and navigable rivers in India, although the former were built largely for irrigation. We get a glimpse of the waterways in Basil Greenhill's *Boats and Boatman of Pakistan* (1971 – Grade B) which describes the author's on-the-spot findings about the river boats of (then both East and West) Pakistan. We can read of an adventurous waterway trip in Eric Newby's *Slowly Down the Ganges* (1966 – Grade B), and can study the development of steam power in Henry Bernstein's *Steamboats on the Ganges* (1960 – Grade C).

Moving further west, we find that the Jordan has attracted a number of navigation attempts, among them one by John MacGregor. He made a lengthy tour, starting with the Nile, followed by a long road haul up through the snows on Mount Lebanon, before reaching the Jordan itself. *The Rob Roy on the Jordan, Nile, Red Sea, and Gennesareth, etc. A canoe cruise in Palestine and Egypt, and the Waters of Damascus* was published in 1869, and a first edition in good condition would be Grade CD. It went into several editions, the most common of which is the eighth, which appeared in 1904 with revisions to both title and text, and is Grade BC. Raven-Hart seems to have overlooked the Jordan, but another Englishman, the Reverend R.J.E.Boggis, Vicar of St John's, Torquay, made a successful descent of the Jordan in 1932. His *Down the Jordan in a Canoe* (1939 – Grade B) also devotes five of its early chapters to describing all the earlier navigation attempts.

The classic works on the Niles are Alan Moorehead's *The Blue Nile* (1962) and *The White Nile* (1960). Both have been much reprinted, but are Grade B in first editions. Raven-Hart's *Canoe Errant on the Nile* (1936 – Grade B) describes his descent from Wadi Halfa, but the first complete descent was not made until 1950/51 by a three-man French expedition. In *4,000 Miles of Adventure: down the Nile by Canoe* (1953 – Grade B) André Davy recounts their many problems, including hippos, and the need to keep away from elevated banks, in case sunbathing crocodiles jumped down onto their heads! Goran Schildt's *The Sun Boat* (1957 – Grade AB) is largely given over to an account of a trip on the

Nile in his yacht *Daphne*, but its closing pages contain a memorable description of their transit of the Sweet Water Canal – an eighty-mile link between the Nile and the Suez Canal. It has a familiar dismal ring to it – a stuck swing bridge, rubbish in the water, and an underwater obstruction which shattered the prop shaft. The canal, locks and all, is primarily a water supply channel and the substantial current made some progress possible, even with no prop, until low water levels found *Daphne* aground amidst a fleet of barges, some of whose skippers revealed that they had been stuck for six days. Finally a tug was conjured up, and dragged *Daphne* to the next lock, bumping her bottom all the way.

Australia is, I think, entirely innocent of navigation canals. However, it does (or did) boast one extensive river navigation system – the 3212 miles of the Murray and its two tributaries, the Darling and the Murrumbidgee. The main river had about twenty-four locks, but navigation on the unlocked tributaries was, at best, seasonal. At the turn of the century, the system supported a fleet of nearly a hundred paddle-steamers and about as many barges, which could be towed by the paddlers. C.E.W.Bean wrote *The 'Dreadnought' of the Darling* (1911 – Grade C) to record a trip down that river, but there aren't many such books around, in England at least. Luckily a publisher and author, Michael Page, co-operated with an old steamer captain, William Drage, to write *Riverboats and Rivermen* published in Adelaide (1976 – Grade B), thus preserving the memories of a lifetime spent on the river, illustrated with many period photographs. Predictably, Raven-Hart couldn't overlook the only major navigation system in the southern hemisphere, and wrote *Canoe in Australia* (Melbourne 1948 – Grade B) after descending the Murrumbidgee and Murray Rivers. The Darling-Murray route would have offered a longer trip, but on arrival in Australia, Raven-Hart found that the Darling was virtually dry, and even he couldn't cope with that.

As far as I know, there are no major navigation canals as such in South America, although some of the rivers have for centuries been used for travelling. I haven't come across any books devoted to these rivers from a navigation viewpoint, although many have supported regular passenger and freight services for years. A single example must suffice – A.S.Wadia's *A Thousand Miles up the Amazon* (1936 – Grade AB) offers no surprise in its tourist's descriptions of the passage up the mighty river to Manaos. What might be a surprise is that his port of embarkation for the *Hilary*, on which he steamed right to Manaos was – Liverpool!

Chapter 7

FICTION

Some of the more solemn collectors reject canal fiction, regarding it as unworthy of serious attention. This is narrow-minded; a novel may not contain facts upon which one would rely, but its very publication is a historical fact, and its portrayal of the waterway scene is an encapsulation of the feelings of the author towards his subject. Taken *en masse*, adult and juvenile fiction tell us a great deal about changing attitudes towards waterways over a period of 150 years, and these attitudes will be sketched out in the remainder of this chapter. Sociology apart, many waterway novels provide us with good entertainment, and are worth reading for that alone.

Adult Fiction

There is something of a shortage of canal fiction written for adults, but this is partly balanced by the fact that amongst their number, waterway novels can boast of two very well known works. These are Jerome K.Jerome's *Three Men in A Boat*, which has a long and distinguished history, and A.P.Herbert's *The Water Gipsies*. Apart from these two, few major authors have taken a waterway theme, or even a waterway background, for any of their books.

Bibliographically, *Three Men in A Boat* offers a lot of mileage, and you will find this fascinating or tedious, depending on whether you are a First Edition Collector or not. It was first published in 1889, but the publisher (Arrowsmith of Bristol) used the date 1889 on the title page for at least 20 years, during which time there were at least 50 impressions. Any copy with '1889' on the title, and no indication that it is a later impression, can be classed as a First. It is, however, widely known that earlier issues have the publisher's address on the title-page as 'Quay Street', whereas later ones have '11 Quay Street'. Much less well known is that sub-types of the 'Quay Street' copies have been identified. Earliest issues have 'J.W.Arrowsmith, Bristol' as the heading to the front paste-down endpaper, and the ornamental initial letters of Chapters 6 and 7 inverted. Second issues have '11 Quay Street, Bristol' on the

The river in its Sunday	The river in its Sunday garb.—Dress on the river.-
for the men.—Abse:	for the men.—Absence of taste in Harris.—Geo1
—A day with th	—A day with the fashion-plate young la
Thomas's tomb.—7	Thomas's tomb.—The man who loves not graves
and skulls.—Harri:	and skulls.—Harris mad.—His views on George
and lemonade.—He	and lemonade.—He performs tricks.

T was
Lock
maze
time ·

T was while passing through
Lock that Harris told me ε
maze experience. It took
time to pass through, as we

Inverted and corrected initial letters from *Three Men in a Boat*.

endpaper, but may be further subdivided into those with the inverted letters, and those without. A mere First, innocent of these finer points, could be as cheap as Grade B, a second state of the second issue would be Grade C, whereas either of the two varieties with inverted letters would reach the dizzy heights of Grade D. Your reaction to these distinctions, and the accompanying price differentials, will enable you to decide what sort of collector you are.

From an early date the book attracted the attentions of pirates in the United States, who apparently sold over a million unauthorised copies. Arrowsmith themselves printed 207,000 copies by March 1909, and reached their 110th impression in 1950, and the book is still in print as a Penguin paperback. The latest addition to the extended history of this highly successful book is the annotated and illustrated edition, published in 1982, with commentary by Christopher Matthew and Benny Green. The sharp-eyed will see that, surprisingly, the title-page reproduced in the book is not from an early issue.

The *Water Gipsies* has a less complicated history, but more than makes up for it by being a far better book. It was first published by Methuen on June 19th 1930, ran to 13 (virtually identical) impressions in the next four years, followed by a few in varying formats, and was later reprinted by Penguin as a paperback. Copies of the first edition are not hard to find at Grade AB, but the dustwrapper is more difficult. It is worth looking for, as it has a pleasing period picture of a narrowboat on the front, and the less pleasing period note˙inside: 'The book is a sympathetic and intimate study of the lives of poor people.'

Having paid homage to the lions, let us now look at the mice. Canal fiction has gone through several phases; one can perhaps distinguish the Romantic (pre-railways), the Moral (directly inspired by George Smith, and therefore confined to the late Victorian period), and then a lacuna until the Revivalist Period which started in the 1950s. This is only a rough mapping, it is true, but it serves to emphasise that the output of canal fiction has been anything but even either in tenor or in volume.

The earliest novel I have yet discovered in which a canal appears is Thomas Love Peacock's *Crotchet Castle*, which was first published in 1831. One can hardly describe it as a 'canal novel'; it is a satire which takes the form of exchanges within a group of people who are, for some reason, embarked upon 'a flotilla of pleasure boats...to carry a choice philosophical party up the Thames and Severn, into the Ellesmere canal...'. The greater part of the journey is condensed into a single sentence (albeit one that stretches to a whole paragraph):

> 'Leaving Lechlade, they entered the canal that connects the Thames with the Severn; ascended by many locks; passed by a tunnel three miles long, through the bowels of Sapperton Hill...continued their navigation into the Ellesmere Canal; moored their pinnaces in the Vale of Llangollen by the aqueduct of Pontycysyllty...'

Irish packet-boat services have already been mentioned in Chapter 1 and it is no surprise to find them incorporated into two early novels: Anthony Trollope's *The Kellys and the O'Kellys* (1848) and Charles Lever's *Jack Hinton the Guardsman* (1844). Neither are very complimentary about the experience of travelling by packet, and a later work of Trollope's shows no great affection for canals either. This is *The Three Clerks* (1858), in which a minor Civil Service Department is parodied as 'The Commissioners of the Internal Navigation', whose employees are known as the 'infernal navvies'. Trollope was himself employed by the General Post Office, and it is clear that it is his own experiences of the Civil Service which are the basis for the parody. All four of these novels would be Grade DE in first edition, but later editions can be found well down Grade A, possibly even under £1. The role of waterways in the four preceding novels is only minor, but such brief references as are made do tell us something of the way in which waterways were regarded at the time. The first novel in which waterways play a major role is William Black's *The Strange Adventures of a House-boat* (1888). This was first published as a serial in the *Illustrated London News* from January to June 1888, and must have proved popular as it went into book form immediately, reaching its 4th edition in 1888, and its 6th (revised) edition in 1890. Novels of the nineteenth century were frequently published in three volumes – now known familiarly as 'three-deckers' – and I think that Black can claim to have written the only waterway three-decker (although Trollope's novels also first appeared as three-deckers). The travels of the horse-drawn house-boat took it up the Thames, onto the Oxford Canal, then via Napton, Warwick, West Hill Tunnel, and Tardebigge, down to the Severn. The return journey to the Thames was accomplished by way of the Thames & Severn. Sufficient detail is given to suggest that the author had personal knowledge of waterways, but the novel as a whole is somewhat slow for modern tastes, and its plot is not dependent upon its waterway setting. Despite having gone into several editions, it is not easily found, and any three-decker version would be Grade CD, and the one-volume revised edition of 1890 is Grade BC.

The first genuine lettered-all-the-way-through canal novel is Amos Reade's *Life in the Cut* of 1889, published as a 'yellow-back', that is to say as a cheap edition, largely intended for sale on railway bookstalls, and therefore graced with an eye-catching pictorial cover. The pictures on the covers of these books were often printed on yellow paper, hence the name. Being cheap, and not designed for a long life, only a very small proportion of the teeming millions has survived, and many of the survivors are in poor condition. Booksellers often group them together, so look along the shelves for Reade; the prize is a highly imaginative novel, which embraces all human life from the country house to the drunken boater, and includes (the subject of the cover picture) a horrible event on the narrow-boat *Waterwitch*:

> '...Jervoise turned sick at what he saw. A smouldering mass of
> alcoholized tissues, the remains of what had been a human form,
> the horror from which this nauseous stench arose, and that pale
> phosphorescence proceeded, lay there before him. Staggering
> from this cremation chamber, Jervoise returned to the tow-path.'

The end of the nineteenth century saw both the Thames and the Broads well established as cruising grounds, and they therefore emerge as subjects for the authors of the day. J.Ashby Sterry's *A Tale of the Thames* (1896) and Fritz Zorn's *Bunce, the Bobby and the Broads* (1900, I guess, though I haven't seen a first edition), are both light-hearted accounts of water holidays, with the former overlain by romance, and the latter by comedy. Neither is easy to come by, and would be Grade B.

A longish gap follows these two; this is not ended by John Remenham's temptingly named *The Canal Mystery* (1928) whose title merely refers to the discovery of a severed head in the Regent's Canal – an early example of the use of a canal for disposal of unwanted objects. 1928 also saw the publication of Howard Keble's *The Fast Gentleman: a tale of the Norfolk Broads* (Grade AB) and Ronald A.Knox's thriller *The Footsteps at the Lock*. I have seen a first edition of this at Grade D, but four cheap editions came out in the next few years, and these ought to be well down Grade A. In 1964, a Penguin edition appeared. However, despite these various editions, it is, like *Strange Adventures of a House-boat,* not easy to find. Where have all those copies gone? Its latest manifestation was as a large-print book in 1978, but even this isn't to be acquired with any ease.

Another thriller of the period is C.P.Snow's *Death Under Sail* (1931 – Grade B), a tale of murder on the Broads, which made it to Penguindom in 1963, and in an allied genre we have L.T.C.Rolt's *Sleep No More: twelve stories of the supernatural* (1948 – Grade BC). Two of the twelve were set on canals and, when reprinted by Branch Line (1974 – Grade AB), the subtitle was altered to *railway, canal and other stories of the supernatural* to make it more attractive to transport enthusiasts. This book may well have been the initial inspiration for Margaret Cornish whose *Still Waters – Mystery Tales of the Canals* was published in 1982.

The post-war novelists have taken a multiplicity of waterway themes reflecting the rise of interest in waterways in recent times. Amongst the dozen or more titles which have been published, we find several set in the canal-building period itself, recreating the violent life of the navvy. Bernard Ash must take the credit for first exploring this world in his *Fitchett's Inn* (1955 – Grade B) which takes a realistic look at the early days of canal building and operation, showing how many country communities were completely transformed by the coming of the canals and the industrialisation which they permitted. Anthony Burton traces this transformation more completely in his trilogy *The Master Idol* (1975), *The Navigators* (1976) and *A Place to Stand* (1977) – all Grade A. In the first, we are introduced to the Tatlows, a family of weavers in Lancashire. In the second, the Tatlow son, Nick, starts as a navvy, but uses his native abilities to become a leader of his fellows, finally ending up as a carrier on the canals in the last of the series. Alexander Cordell also takes a historical theme, but chooses the early nineteenth century for *The Song of the Earth* (1969 – Grade A) a marvellously colourful tale of the reaction of a boat family in South Wales to the coming of the railways. A.P.Herbert shows us his love for the Thames sailing barge in *The Singing Swan* (1968 – Grade B), an uneven novel whose wealth of detail of barge sailing will delight some and bore others. Ngaio Marsh adds another thriller to our list: *Clutch of Constables* (1968 – Grade A), an unremarkable story of skulduggery on a hotel boat on imaginary waterways in East Anglia. I can't resist closing on *Young Adam* (AB) by Alexander Trocchi, first published in Paris in 1954, and recently re-issued as a paperback by Calder, which describes the life of an unprincipled barge-hand on the Forth & Clyde. It must surely be the only canal novel to appear within the famous sage-green wrappers of the Olympia Press.

Children's Fiction

For some reason which escapes me, there is far more canal fiction written for children than for their parents. Since the war, stories for children have outnumbered those for adults by three or four to one. The majority are unremarkable, and a few are poor, likely to provide adults with no more pleasure than spotting the numerous mistakes with which their text and illustrations are peppered.

During the late nineteenth century, a number of publishers produced children's books specifically intended for school prizes, particularly for Sunday Schools. These were cheaply made, although within hard covers, and achieved economy by the use of standard bindings, and often re-using existing (and not always appropriate) printing blocks for illustrations. There must have been millions, but time has dealt harshly with them, as it has with the yellow-backs, and almost all the survivors are in poor condition. They almost invariably tell tales with strong moral or religious themes, in which Good, assisted by Faith, triumphs over Evil and Adversity. It is in this group that the first children's waterway books are found.

Many of these books were published anonymously, and are undated. Both are true for *Between the Locks: or the adventures of a water-party* (B), which was actually written by the Reverend Edward Hoare, Vicar of Stoneycroft, and published by the Society for Promoting Christian Knowledge, in about 1877. It tells of a family group who go up the Medway in a small boat for a holiday, only to end up evangelising amongst the hop-pickers. This sort of theme was common enough, but on the waterfront was given a renewed impetus by the work of George

Smith who was busy building up a public image of the boatman as a drunken dissolute illiterate, brutal to his overworked wife and to his numerous starving children. Ideal raw material was how the 'prize writers' saw it, and in the 1880s and 1890s a small but coherent group of books appeared, directly inspired by George Smith. The most well known, because later writers have used its illustrations, is *Rob Rat: a story of barge life.* It was written by Mark Pearse, although some editions have his name on the front cover but not on the title page, and was probably first published in 1877 or 1878. It is now very rare, and would be Grade C, and it is difficult to believe that 31,000 copies were produced, yet I have seen a copy with 'Thirty-first thousand' proudly printed on the title page. The other members of this small group would all be Grade BC, and they include Annie Gray's *The Old Lock Farm* (c.1888) and Emma Leslie's *Tom the Boater* (c.1882), both authors being prolific writers of prize books. Another well known writer of these moral tales was L.T.Meade, whose *Water Gipsies, or the adventures of Rag, Tag and Bobtail* was published in 1879 in New York under the sub-title *A story of canal life in England*, but did not appear in book form in England until several years later. It seems that the Americans pirated the story from an English magazine, in which it had been published in 1878, a common practice of the period. Taken together, the moral tales now form a pretty elusive bunch of books, and yet they must have done a lot to shape a whole generation's views of life on canals.

The idea that waterway settings were appropriate for 'improving tales' seems to have lived on, at least for the Broads, for we find Percy F.Westerman's *A Mystery of the Broads* (c.1930 – Grade B) and two books by Morgan Derham, both Grade A, published by the Children's Special Service Mission: *On the Trail of the Windward* (1948) and *The Cruise of the Clipper* (1952). Two of Arthur Ransome's excellent stories also take place in Broadland: *Coot Club* (1934) and *The Big Six* (1940). Reprints of Ransome abound, at Grade A, but devotees are beginning to collect the first editions which are now moving into Grade B.

Returning to canals proper, not all the books take a cruise as story. Robert M.Bateman's *Canoe Boy* (1967) sees a local derelict canal as restorable by volunteers for canoeing. John Verney's *Friday's Tunnel* (1959) doesn't actually involve navigation at all, but the tunnel is an old canal tunnel, first recognised as such by Robin, a student with a green duffel coat and purple suede shoes, who is 'writing an essay on canals' for his degree. The tunnel, of course, hides all sorts of secrets in this exciting and imaginative adventure story.

Susan Woolfitt, rightly famed for *Idle Women* (see Chapter 3), is less well known as the author of *Escape to Adventure* (1948 – Grade B), a tale of the Grand Union, which draws on her first-hand knowledge of the cut. One or two established children's writers have included canal stories amongst their output. I have in mind Malcolm Saville with *The Riddle of the Painted Box* (1947 – Grade AB), *Two Fair Plaits* (1948 – Grade AB) and *Young Johnnie Bimbo* (1956 – Grade AB), and Noel Streatfeild's *Thursday's Child* (1970 – Grade A). This was televised, which presumably boosted sales of the paperback edition which first appeared in 1972. Brian Wright's *The Canal Children* (1976 – Grade A) is the book of a television serial telling a lively tale of the Warwick & Birmingham Canal in the 1840s. For a real change of viewpoint, turn up C.Fraser-Simson's *Canal Cats* (1955 – Grade A), whose hero is a kitten who jumps aboard a narrow boat on the Regent's Canal.

Foreign Fiction

Doubtless, fiction of the sort described so far in this chapter exists in many other countries, but few books published in Britain take foreign waterways as a theme. Erskine Childers' *The Riddle of the Sands* (1903 – Grade D) just about qualifies, as canals and barges play a significant role in the plot. Charles Maurice Chenu wrote *My Canoe* in French, but an English translation was published by the Scholartis Press in 1931, and would now be Grade B. Alexander Trocchi's *Cain's Book* (1963 – Grade AB) describes the life of a scowman working on the east coast of the USA. A scow is an unpowered barge, with a capacity of several hundred tons, and it is in the cabin of a working scow that Trocchi's leading character lives his dissolute life, almost free from interference from the land. The early days of the canals in North America would seem to offer plenty of scope to the novelist, but I think that no Englishman has yet taken the opportunity. I do know of one American novel of the prosperous days of the Erie Canal: *Rome Haul* (1929 – Grade B) by Walter Edmonds.

When the internal combustion engine first came to the canals, threatening to oust the horse, there were doubtless many boatmen who resisted the change, seeing their days out with horses (or donkeys) because they believed in the 'rightness' of the older ways. The theme is a recognisable one, and one which has been used in at least one film. However, the earlier paddle-steamer versus horse-barge confrontation is one which probably had little expression in Britain. On the larger rivers of Europe, however, the introduction of the paddle-tug played havoc with the traditional barge traffic, as Bernard Clavel portrays so graphically in his novel *Lord of the River* (1972). The English translation (AB) was published in 1973. Do read it if you get the chance; it is evocative, powerful and moving, and in my view the best waterway novel yet written.

French waterways also provide the setting for two of George Simenon's crime stories: *Le Charretier de la 'Providence'* and *L'Ecluse No. 1'*. Both of these thrillers revolve around boats and boatmen, and both have been translated into English. The first translation of the former was *The Crime at Lock 14* published in *The Triumph of Inspector Maigret* by Hurst & Blackett in 1934. Nearly thirty years later, Penguin produced a new translation – *Maigret Meets a Milord* (1963 – Grade A). The title refers to an English aristocrat, travelling in his yacht on the French canals. *L'Ecluse No 1* was included as *The Lock at Charenton* in *Maigret Sits It Out* published in 1941 by Routledge. A third Simenon story, *The House by the Canal* (1952), although set on a Belgian canal, is not intimately based on canal life, as the first two are.

Juvenile fiction set on waterways abroad is almost as sparse as that for adults. Roger Pilkington, with characteristic energy, has written five books describing the adventures of the Branxome family aboard the *Dabchick*, in which they enjoy a number of waterway holidays in Europe. Almost a 'Small Boat' series for small readers, each has an authentic waterway setting ranging from France to Scandinavia. *Jan's Treasure* (1955) was the first, quickly followed by *The Chesterfield Gold* (1957), *The Missing Panel* (1958), *The Dahlia's Cargo* (1959), and *Don John's Ducats* (1960). All are Grade A, as is G.W.Barrington's *Jan: the story of a Dutch Barge Dog* (1956), which ran to at least five impressions.

The Mississippi will, of course, always be remembered for the memorable raft journey in Mark Twain's *The Adventures of Huckleberry Finn*, first published in Boston in 1883. The Great Lakes are the 'inland waters' in *Elsie's journey on inland waters* (1895 – Grade A), a rather tedious work in the 'Elsie' series of 'High-class books for Girls, specially suited for Sunday School Prizes', and even the Panama Canal is not forgotten, if we include *The Boy Scouts at the Panama Canal* (A) by Lieutenant Howard Payson, published in New York in 1913, *before* the opening of the canal. In this stirring tale, the Scouts foil a plot to blow up the Gatun Dam, which surely shows that for an ingenious author the choice of a canal setting need place no curb on the imagination.

Chapter 8

EPHEMERA, POSTCARDS, AND OTHER BITS AND PIECES

Almost by definition, the range of ephemeral printed material relating to waterways is too great for me to do more than hint at a few examples. One of the great pleasures of collecting ephemera is that your own collection is unique, and certainly not to be found neatly catalogued in any library. Confining present remarks to printed material, what might the collector find? Obviously, the canal companies, carriers and contractors all issued printed material of one sort or another, and many examples survive. *The Canals of the British Isles* series and the *Inland Waterway Histories* series both use such material for text illustrations, and are well worth scrutinising for this alone. Thus we find posters advertising various canal services, posters forbidding all sorts of misbehaviour (including swimming in the canal, or riding bicycles on the towpath), toll tickets, share certificates, invoices, and all the predictable ephemera produced by public companies carrying on their day-to-day business. Of course not all collectable ephemera was produced by the canal companies – take, for example, the series of London Transport posters of the 1920s and 1930s showing commercial and pleasure craft on the Grand Union Canal and Thames (EF).

To illustrate the variety of ephemera which does exist, I will just list a few items which have recently come to hand: a set of six trade cards, issued by Liebig in 1903, depicting canal scenes in colour (B), an official invitation to attend the demonstration of BACAT in the Thames in 1974 (A), *I-SPY Boats and Waterways* a 48-page booklet published by the *News Chronicle* in about 1955 (A), a map published by the Barge Mission of the Diocese of Lichfield in 1877, showing the most popular tying-up places for boatmen (A), and a set of 12 small photos of the Caledonian Canal published by Valentine in about 1910, enclosed in a tartan packet (A). Raw material for historians is not confined to Minute Books and Acts of Parliament!

Newspaper cuttings can also help to recreate the past – I once found a scrap of the *Evening News* down the side of an old armchair which turned out to include the whole of an article, dated 4 May 1928, titled 'The Canals that Nobody Wants', explaining that the railway companies felt that ownership of one third of the canal system had been forced upon them, and that the responsibility for these was so onerous that 'we cannot even *give* them away!'

Without doubt, the most popular type of canal ephemera, and the most readily available, is the postcard. The early years of this century saw an explosion of the postcard industry, and although canals held no obvious appeal for our grandfathers, who were unlikely to be very interested in them either commercially or scenically, and who didn't regard them as suitable for cruising, the search for new subjects naturally led the postcard publishers to issue many postcards of waterway scenes. Some of these are of very high quality, printed in colour or black and white, and the fact that many have been subsequently reproduced as book illustrations is eloquent testimony to their value as historical records. Some of the picture books referred to in Chapter 3 contain numerous examples, but the only book given over to a study of the canal postcard *per se* is Hugh McKnight's *Waterways Postcards 1900-1930* (1983).

It is tempting to think that ephemera must be 'old' to be interesting enough to collect. However, many of today's printed items, virtually throwaways, are worth consideration. It has been pointed out many times that today's commonplace is tomorrow's rarity. Thus stamps depicting canals have their adherents, as do modern postcards, BWB calendars, IWA Rally Brochures, even hire boat brochures. Although many of these are unexciting in ones and twos, an organised collection can be of interest and value. Tom Rolt once wrote an introduction to a hire boat brochure, and Robert Aickman did the same for more than one IWA Rally brochure. The passage of time has made these slight pamphlets into objects of some interest – provided somebody's still got one or two for the historian to look at!

Prints, quite definitely, are not ephemera, for many were produced to be permanent pictorial records, but as they are often sold by dealers in ephemera, it makes sense to include them here. I have neither the knowledge nor the inclination to embark upon a discussion of the various techniques of printing, with the necessary distinctions between copper plates, steel engravings, wood engravings etc. For our purposes, it will be enough to note that most of the prints the canal collector will come across will be steel engravings from the late eighteenth and early nineteenth centuries, or wood engravings from the mid-nineteenth century to about the first World War. The majority of these were published in books or magazines, and this gives rise to argument, particularly in the case of books. There are some who maintain that a book is a book, and that it is a despicable act to remove its illustrations in order to sell them off individually. Others reply by pointing out that many books are so expensive that few can afford them, so that selling off their contents piecemeal spreads the goodies further. A cynical observer has remarked that as the argument is incapable of resolution to the satisfaction of both parties, it will continue until there are no plate books left. This at least conveys the salutory warning that breaking is effectively a one-way process; there are comparatively few instances of someone collecting separated plates to restore a book to its original state.

Some prints were hand-coloured before being bound up in their books, but most of the earlier coloured prints now offered for sale have been coloured recently, usually immediately after being broken out. Thus the description 'Original hand-coloured print, guaranteed at least a hundred years old' is a carefully chosen phrase, and one which does *not* in fact guarantee the age of the colouring itself. Plain or coloured, it is undeniable that many make attractive decorations, although one must always remember that as historical records they are less than reliable. The original artist often changed or omitted details of the scene, and the engraver may well have made further modifications. The same is, of course, true for photographs and postcards, but they are in fact far less frequently tampered with, and therefore are better raw material for the historian. Many bookshops, antique dealers, and art dealers sell prints as well, often for only a few pounds if unframed, and the collector would do well to avoid buying framed prints if possible. He will thus be able to commission framing and mounts to suit his own taste, and will be able to inspect the print closely for details of its condition (do make sure it has not been stuck down by a vandal with sellotape or lashings of glue) and record any details of publisher, engraver or artist, which may well get covered up by the mount.

Although there is only one canal book illustrated with colour plates, John Hassell's *Tour of the Grand Junction Canal* (1819 – Grade G), a wide variety of canal prints may be found. Earlier ones are generally landscapes showing canals, but later examples include more details of the canals, boats and boaters themselves. The *Graphic* and the *Illustrated London News* have yielded a number of wood engravings of canal scenes, including several depicting the results of the explosion on

84

the Regent's Canal in 1874. *The Gentleman's Magazine* contained a few canal pictures from time to time, and also a number of canal maps. Encyclopedias are also broken up for their illustrations, and these may of course include some depicting canals. The sources are, in short, fairly extensive, and the collector's problem is likely to be the selection of a theme for a collection, rather than locating interesting material.

In strong distinction to the print collector, the numismatist has little scope for canal themes, if he is sticking to British coins and medals. There are just a handful of canal tokens, and commemorative medallions for the Manchester Ship Canal and the Gloucester & Berkeley. The tokens display a variety which compensates for the comparatively few issues which exist. Several show canal scenes in some detail, including, for example, Sapperton Tunnel, Ketley Inclined Plane, and Gloucester Docks. Most were issued by the canal or river navigation companies themselves, but on the Basingstoke Canal the contractor, John Pinkerton, issued tokens to pay his navvies. Most tokens are of copper, although silver was occasionally also used.

This being a book about books, it would not do to stray too far into the world of collectable hardware. There is, however, plenty of scope for the canal collector, both in modern items and antiques. The world of ceramics is represented in several ways; there are canal age commemorative mugs and plates, there are the celebrated lace plates, Measham teapots and other Measham pieces (these being *de rigeur* amongst narrow-boaters) and there are recent items, such as the plates issued to commemorate the centenary of the Anderton Lift. The IWA has developed a system of giving metal plaques for boats attending rallies; similar plaques are also awarded by some local canal societies to boats navigating to particular defined points on the system, Slough Basin for example. Such plaques are obviously eminently collectable. Once into canal oddments, the list is endless: painted utensils and other objects decorated with 'roses and castles', miniature windlasses, boat horse harness, recorded canal songs, and (for the museum or very wealthy collector) engines, and even the boats themselves.

Chapter 9

A NOTE ON THE FINDING, SELECTION AND CARE OF BOOKS

Finding a supplier for books which are in print presents no great problem; your local bookshop is the obvious first choice. If this doesn't answer your need, then one or other of the specialist postal services can be used. There are two of these, one run by the Inland Waterways Association, the other by *Waterways World*. Neither stocks all the titles in print, only the better sellers, and remember that their list prices are higher than the publishers' prices, to cover post and packing. This is particularly punitive if a number of books are being bought simultaneously. Your local canal society or IWA branch may run a bookstall at meetings and rallies; buying your books from their bookstall will avoid postal charges, and swell their funds. All these sources are bound by trade agreements not to reduce prices below those fixed by the publishers, books being almost the only products still sold at prices fixed by the producer, not the individual retailer. However, from time to time special opportunities do occur, in the shape of remainders or other cut-price offers, and you may also find that one of these organisations has a stock of items which are out of print, and therefore not available through normal channels.

Most of the world's books are out of print; the acquisition of these presents more of a challenge, and the chase is more fun. Secondhand books may be hunted, and found, in a vast range of places from bookshops to jumble sales, from market stalls to junk shops. The excitement lies in never knowing with certainty whether a particular shop or jumble sale is worth a visit or not. It probably isn't, but we all know the satisfying glow which comes from having discovered some sought-after rarity in an unlikely spot – a pile of tired school texts, sermons and AA books *may* conceal a copy of *Maidens' Trip*, an unpretentious jumble sale may have been favoured by your local book reviewer discarding a few review copies. Perhaps the most unlikely books I've ever bought from a jumble sale were two eighteenth-century books about Scotland, with auctioneers' markers (Christies', as I recall) still tucked into the front. The full calf in which they had been bound was worn, to say the least, and that explained the wrinkled nose of the charming lady behind the stall, when I asked her how much they were. 'They're rather old' she said distastefully 'so I suppose 5p is about right'. 'Each, of course' she added, not wishing to undervalue them.

Surprises there may be, but in most secondhand bookshops, the inquirer after canal books will be told that 'they're very difficult to get – but have a look in the maritime section, you might find something'. Indeed you might, but there will come a time when, although you don't stop hunting in the unlikely places, you will want to turn to a bookdealer who specialises in books on canals, or in some other related field such as maritime or industrial history. Their prices will almost undoubtedly be higher than those of a general secondhand bookshop, but their stock is likely to contain those rarer items which are difficult to find elsewhere. Several guides to secondhand booksellers and their specialities exist (see Chapter 10) but they become out-of-date very quickly. Active specialist dealers will usually advertise in the appropriate magazines; for present purposes that means *Waterways World*, *IWA Waterways*, and, to a lesser extent, *Canal & Riverboat*. The selection of books is not a subject on which any writer can lay down guidelines; it is entirely up to the collector what he collects, and which copies he regards as worth having. There are no hard and fast rules. One man may have the patience and cash to pursue the finest copy of the first edition, another may quite properly be content with a tatty Book Club edition, or a copy with a couple of illustrations missing, but with a complete text. However, with one of those twists which are meat and drink to logicians, I wish to state one hard and fast rule: First is not necessarily Best. I say this because of the rapid rise in prices asked (I would not say values) for what are collectively known as Modern Firsts – which really means first impressions of first editions of those 20th-century novelists, poets and playwrights who are currently in vogue amongst the wealthier book-collectors. Thus hundreds (yes, hundreds) of pounds may be asked for a first edition of *Watership Down*, *Casino Royale*, or *The Tale of Peter Rabbit*. There is a slight tendency for the idea that First is Best to creep into non-fiction as well – and it is largely non-fiction which concerns the canal man. Resist this idea, and think for yourself. Take, for example, a book like Hadfield's *Canals of the West Midlands*. This was first published in 1966, and a second edition appeared in 1969, in which a number of corrections were made. As this is primarily a reference book, the second edition is to be preferred to the first. If, instead, we look at Hadfield's *British Canals*, which has already gone to seven editions, it remains true that the latest edition is the best, as its coverage is greater than its predecessors. However, the passage of time has now begun to impart some interest to the first edition. One wouldn't buy it for reference, but to be able to handle, to experience this pioneering book, whose publication led (whatever the author might have thought at the time) to the establishment of the publishing company of David & Charles. It has, in short, become a publication of some significance. A collector, then, might quite logically choose to collect the first and the last editions of *British Canals*.

Conversely, with a book like Phillips' *General History of Inland Navigation*, the 'first and last' approach would not be sound. As we have seen in Chapter 2, the third edition is probably the most desirable, containing more information than the first two, and being more handsome than the later two. In addition, it is possible to acquire a facsimile of the fifth edition, which will be a lot cheaper than any of the originals. Some collectors eschew facsimiles as being second-best; before following suit, remember that some facsimiles carry very informative prefaces, from which we may learn about the original author and his life, the publishing history of the book, or its strengths and shortcomings. The writer of such a preface may even extend the coverage of the book, e.g. the bibliographic material in the facsimile of Jackman's *Development of Transportation in Modern England*, or include extra illustrations, as in the case of the David & Charles edition of Thurston's *Flower of Gloster*. All in all, the collector must consider each book as a separate case, and decide what for him is the most desirable.

Books signed by their authors are more common than one might at first expect. An author's signature certainly adds interest to a book, but doesn't necessarily increase its cash value. If the author is a minor figure, or even a major one known to have been a prolific signer, then the presence of a signature alone will not add to its worth. If it includes a dedication or other personal comment, particularly to a person connected with the book or well known in their own right, then the value may be increased. In this category, I have seen £75 asked for a battered copy of A.P.Herbert's *No Boats on the River* (1932 – Grade C) which had been given to Stanley Baldwin, then leader of the Conservative Party. Ideally, a signed copy will also be dated, and preferably dated soon after publication. Occasionally dedications may be found dated 10 or 20 years after publication, which suggests the author was slowly working through unsold stock by giving it away. Besides authors' signatures other inscriptions or marks of ownership may lend both interest and value. Books may be found stamped by the Grand Union Canal Company, for instance, and I have two (Parliamentary) Bills for the Calder & Hebble, each stamped by the Aire & Calder Navigation, and with Priestley's name in a firm clear hand in the corner. There are even bookplates featuring canals – I have seen a charming canal scene at Berkhamsted – which suggests to the dedicated that a collection of waterway bookplates might be a possibility.

Once chosen (by whatever criteria) and acquired, books must be cared for. Many useful books have been written on this subject, some of which are mentioned in Chapter 10. I will not trespass on the preserve of wiser and more experienced writers, but will just leave you with a Golden Rule – Avoid doing anything to a book which is irreversible. In particular, don't use any but water-soluble glues for minor repairs (including repairs to dustwrappers), and PLEASE NEVER USE SELLOTAPE. Librarians love to swap tales of crimes perpetrated on books by readers – my favourite being the one about the man who used a piece of bacon as a bookmark – but in my experience more books are irreversibly marred by the use of sellotape than by any other single cause. Library staff, I regret to say, are high on the list of such despoilers; don't add yourself to their number.

Author's signature from *A Caravan Afloat*.

Chapter 10

HOW TO FIND OUT MORE

The preceding pages have done no more than pick out a few of the highlights of the literature; fairly soon the collector or historian will feel the need for something more substantial, more complete. There is as yet no good bibliography of the subject – nothing within shouting distance of Ottley's famous *A Bibliography of British Railway History* (1965) whose drift to the top of Grade D was rudely reversed by the announcement of plans for a new edition. Several lesser listings have been published, the most useful of which are those in Charles Hadfield's *British Canals* and Edward Paget-Tomlinson's *The Complete Book of Canal & River Navigations* (1978). The seventh edition of *British Canals* (1984) devotes five pages to a bibliography, comprising nearly 200 items published in Britain, almost all of which are books. Unfortunately, the entries are very brief, merely giving author, title, and date of publication, and occasionally adding the word 'reprinted' when a facsimile or other modern edition has later appeared. Paget-Tomlinson's bibliography contains about twice as many entries, including many from periodicals, but gives little more detail than Hadfield, although a few items have very brief comments for the reader's guidance. For a more comprehensive but early bibliography, reference should be made to Jackman's two-volume *The Development of Transportation in Modern England* (1916), with its 62 pages listing about 1500 sources of all sorts. Remember, though, that this total includes all forms of inland transport, and that 'modern' means up to about 1850.

The most comprehensive compilation to date is the one I have built up on a computer file at Imperial College, London. This contains about 1500 entries covering books and booklets published in the English language, relating to all aspects of navigable waterways, worldwide. Each entry contains the following elements: Author, Title, Place of Publication, Publisher, Date, Pagination (including illustrations etc), and, where appropriate, notes to clarify the contents of obscurely titled works, and on subsequent editions (if any). Each entry also carries a set of codes summarising all the important details, thus allowing automatic searches to be made through the file to locate and list all books on particular subjects published at or between specified dates. It is necessary to charge a small fee for access to this file; full details may be obtained from:

> Dr Mark Baldwin
> Civil Engineering Department
> Imperial College
> London SW7 2BU

A brief account of this, and other computer-based storage and retrieval systems, may be found on pages 21-24 of the *Journal of the Railway and Canal Historical Society* for November 1981.

Using the computer file as a starting point, I have compiled a bibliography of waterways in the British Isles, for publication in 1984. This lists, under seven main subheadings, about 700 books and booklets on waterways, including fiction, published in Britain in or before 1950. It will be published in a *Festschrift* in honour of Charles Hadfield, entitled *Canals – A New Look*. The book has six other contributors, working under the editorship of Tony Burton and myself. Two other shorter bibliographies are provided – one on the works of Charles Hadfield (of which 80 entries relate to waterways), and the other on accounts of small boat cruises on the European mainland published in or before 1939, of which there are about 80. Thus the book will contain, in addition to the informative contributions by leading canal writers, three bibliographies totalling nearly 900 entries, and this constitutes a major step forward in the study of the subject.

The nearest thing to a general world book catalogue is the enormous *National Union Catalogue*, whose main section runs to nearly 700 volumes. This does not relate to a single library, but comprises the combined catalogues of all the important libraries in the USA and Canada. It is, of course, particularly strong on English language publications, and its history means that it is a much more thorough catalogue of different editions of each book than is our own *British Library Catalogue*. This is also a massive work, although considerably smaller than the *NUC*, and is the prime general source of information on books published in Britain, at least up to 1950. Nevertheless, the *NUC* often contains far more entries for a particular author, even a British one. Both of these major catalogues are primarily author indexes, and although they are supplemented by subject catalogues, these are rather patchy. This really means that, before you start, you've got to know what to look for. Since 1950, the research becomes easier, as the *British*

National Bibliography comes on the scene, and this has a more thorough approach to subject indexing, and also lists books by title as well as by author. It is, of course, not retrospective, nor is it cumulative, which means that a particular subject must be pursued through numerous volumes, usually one per year, which isn't too bad in the 1980s, but will be an increasingly daunting task as the years roll by. *British Books in Print* is a useful 2-volume reference work, published annually, giving (both by author and title) details of current books; current and past issues can be useful if, for instance, you know the title of a book and wish to discover its author.

So much for the more comprehensive sources of information. For particular topics, other possibilities exist. **Civil Engineering** is well served by the Institution of Civil Engineers, who have issued numerous printed indexes to their own publications, and of their library holdings. The library is not open to the public, but may be used by non-members making written application. *Early Printed Reports and Maps (1665 – 1850) in the Library of the Institution of Civil Engineers* (1977) is the title of a useful book by Professor Skempton, containing details of hundreds of these elusive items, including over a hundred on canals and river navigations.

Cruises on inland waterways are one of the pre-occupations of the Cruising Association, and they have issued six printed catalogues of their library, the latest being *Supplement 1954 – 1980*. The library is not open to non-members. Bibliographies may also be found in Paul Vine's *Pleasure Boating in the Victorian Era* (Phillimore, 1983) and *Canals – a New Look* (see above).

Tokens are placed in their social context by J.R.S.Whiting's *Trade Tokens: a social and economic history* (1971 – Grade A), which illustrates and describes most of the British canal and river navigation tokens. The standard numismatic works on trade tokens are *The Provincial Token-Coinage of the 18th Century illustrated* (3 vols: 1910 – 1918) by R.Dalton and S.H.Hamer, and *The Nineteenth Century Token Coinage of Great Britain, Ireland, the Channel Islands and the Isle of Man* (1904) by W.J.Davis.

Prints are dealt with in some detail in R.V.Tooley's *English Books with Coloured Plates, 1790 – 1860: Bibliographical Accounts of the Most Important Books Illustrated by English Artists in Colour Aquatint and Colour Lithography* (Dawson, reprinted 1979), although many prints with canal interest fall outside its terms of reference. A general book on the subject is Ronald Russell's *Guide to British Topographical Prints* (1979 – Grade B).

Inland Shipping, a term given wide circulation by the IWA, may be pursued via the bibliography in *British Freight Waterways Today & Tomorrow* (IWA, 1980) which lists nearly 100 relevant books, papers and periodicals.

Bookshop Guides are essential for the committed book-hunter, but have the disadvantage of going out of date rather rapidly. The most comprehensive is *A Directory of Dealers in Secondhand and Antiquarian Books in the British Isles*, published every three years by the Sheppard Press. A new edition is due in 1984, and is a worthwhile investment, as a large number of the dealers listed work from private premises, and are thus not to be discovered by prowling around the streets. A similar *Annual Directory of Booksellers in the British Isles specialising in Antiquarian and Out-of-print books* is published by The Clique. Shops alone are discussed in *The Book Browser's Guide: Britain's Secondhand and Antiquarian Bookshops* (1975 – Grade A).

Book Collecting and Book Care are dealt with by Seamus Stewart in *Book Collecting: a beginner's guide* (David & Charles, 2nd edition 1979). The greatest modern authority is John Carter, author of several works for the bookman, notably *ABC for Book-Collectors* (Granada, 5th edition 1981) and *Taste and Technique in Book-collecting* (1974 – Grade B).

Libraries

Under the 'LASER' scheme, each major public library in south-east England has agreed to specialise in a particular subject area, in addition to maintaining the stocks and services expected of a public library. The intention is that these special collections are to be regarded as forming, in aggregate, a huge regional library, far more comprehensive than the resources of any individual borough would allow. The subject areas of these special collections are defined by Dewey numbers; most inland waterway books are catalogued at 386. From 1950 to 1975 the library collecting material in the range 380 – 389 was **Holborn Central Library**, 32 Theobald's Road, London WC1, and this library still has a good waterway stock. In 1976, responsibility for collecting 380 – 389 passed to **Hertfordshire County Library**. However, the county stock is dispersed throughout the various branch libraries, and no central waterway stock or catalogue is available.

Under the British Library Act 1972, the **British Library** was formed in 1973 by amalgamating various existing libraries, the most important of which was the British Museum Library, with its famous circular Reading Room. It owes an enormous part of its collection to the various Copyright Acts, which compel publishers to send to the library, free of charge, one copy of every new publication. Admission to the Reading Room is open to all, but formal application must be made, and a reader's ticket obtained. Most newspapers and other periodicals are held at the British Library's premises at Colindale, and may be consulted there. Government papers, Acts etc. can be seen in the Official Publication Library (previously the State Papers Room) in the British Museum, or at the **House of Lords Records Office** (formal application required).

Many books written since 1947 refer to the British Transport Historical Records at Porchester Road, Paddington. This was an archive established by the British Transport Commission to house the records of the numerous companies they took over on 1 January 1948. Other BTC archives were set up in York and Edinburgh. The Paddington collection, together with material from York not duplicated at Paddington, has now been transferred to the **Public Record Office** at Kew. The Edinburgh collection is now administered by the **Scottish Record Office**. Formal application is required for access to both of these.

The **Science Museum Library** at South Kensington has good collections of historical material and periodicals, and is open to the public without formality.

At **Leicester University** the transport history collection, established in 1953, has now grown to become a major library for the study of transport history, and may be used by members of the public on formal application. Although particularly strong on railways, the collection does contain a lot of waterway material.

Mention has already been made of the fact that the libraries of the **Cruising Association** and **Institution of Civil Engineers** are for members only, but that permission may be given to non-members wishing to use these libraries. In contrast, the libraries of the **British Waterways Board** and the **Inland Waterways Association** are not available for public consultation at all.

INDEX of PERSONS

Numbers in **bold** type refer to illustrations.

INDEX of SUBJECTS

Numbers in **bold** type refer to illustrations.

The country's largest stock of antiquarian, out-of-print, and second-hand waterway books is held by

M & M BALDWIN

**98 Kenyon Street,
LONDON SW6 6LB**
Tel: 01-385 2036

We sell books on all other aspects of transport and industrial history, too. If you would like to receive a copy of our next catalogue, please let us know what subjects you're interested in, and enclose a stamped, self-addressed envelope (preferably big enough to take an A5 catalogue – about 6½ by 8½ inches).

*Visitors welcome, but
BY APPOINTMENT ONLY,
please.*

PUBLISHERS OF INLAND WATERWAYS BOOKS

AND POSTCARDS

Additionally, we sell by Mail Order
most in-print Inland Waterways Books
and Maps. For £1·00 (stamps, refund-
able on first purchase) we will send
an Illustrated Catalogue of titles
ranging from the British Isles to
Europe, the U.S.A. and Australia.
New books are added constantly. This
must be the easiest way to buy from
a huge and fascinating stock which
is probably the biggest anywhere.

THE CLOCK HOUSE, UPPER HALLIFORD, SHEPPERTON, MIDDLESEX TW17 8RU
TELEPHONE: SUNBURY-ON-THAMES 83319

Personal callers: appointment only